THE ASSESSMENT
AND MANAGEMENT
OF SUICIDALITY

M. David Rudd, PhD, ABPP

Texas Tech University

D1560046

Professional Resource Press
Sarasota, Florida

Published by
Professional Resource Press
(An imprint of Professional Resource Exchange, Inc.)
Post Office Box 3197
Sarasota, FL 34230-3197

Printed in the United States of America

Copyright © 2006
by Professional Resource Exchange, Inc.

This publication is sold with the understanding that the publisher is not engaged in rendering professional services. If legal, psychological, medical, accounting, or other expert advice or assistance is sought or required, the reader should seek the services of a competent professional.

The copy editor for this book was Patricia Rockwood, the managing editor was Debbie Fink, the production coordinator was Laurie Girsch, and the typesetter was Richard Sullivan.

Library of Congress Cataloging-in-Publication Data

Rudd, M. David, date.
    The assessment and management of suicidality / M. David Rudd.
       p. cm. -- (Practitioner's resource series)
    Includes bibliographical references.
    ISBN-13: 978-1-56887-105-9 (alk. paper)
    ISBN-10: 1-56887-105-8 (alk. paper)
     1. Suicide--Risk factors. 2. Suicide--Prevention. I. Title. II. Series.

RC569.R828 2006
616.85'8445--dc22

2006047361

<u>DEDICATION</u>

*To all the hard working clinicians willing
to see high-risk suicidal patients.*

SERIES PREFACE

As a publisher of books, multimedia materials, and continuing education programs, the Professional Resource Press strives to provide mental health professionals with highly applied resources that can be used to enhance clinical skills and expand practical knowledge.

All of the titles in the Practitioner's Resource Series are designed to provide important new information on topics of vital concern to psychologists, clinical social workers, marriage and family therapists, psychiatrists, and other mental health professionals.

Although the focus and content of each title in this series will be quite different, there will be notable similarities:

1. Each title in the series will address a timely topic of critical clinical importance.
2. The target audience for each title will be practicing mental health professionals. Our authors were chosen for their ability to provide concrete "how-to-do-it" guidance to colleagues who are trying to increase their competence in dealing with complex clinical problems.
3. The information provided in these titles will represent "state-of-the-art" information and techniques derived from both clinical experience and empirical research. Each of these guidebooks will include references and resources for those who wish to pursue more advanced study of the discussed topics.
4. The authors will provide numerous case studies, specific recommendations for practice, and the types of "nitty-gritty" details that clinicians need before they can incorporate new concepts and procedures into their practices.

We feel that one of the unique assets of Professional Resource Press is that all of its editorial decisions are made by mental health professionals. The publisher, all editorial consultants, and all reviewers are practicing psychologists, marriage and family therapists, clinical social workers, and psychiatrists.

If there are other topics you would like to see addressed in this series, please let me know.

Lawrence G. Ritt, Publisher

ABSTRACT

Targeting suicide risk assessment and management, this book is written in a readable and succinct style purposefully intended for clinicians and clinicians-in-training. The book offers a specific and empirically grounded approach to suicide risk assessment and subsequent management decisions. Although compact, it is thorough and detailed, providing the practitioner with a solid foundation for one of the most challenging areas in clinical practice. The book includes easy-to-follow procedures (with specific questions) for detailed assessment of suicidal thinking, along with related risk factors. It also incorporates several printed forms that organize the assessment data in a manner that helps ease the clinical charting process. Overall, the book provides the clinician with a compact but thorough reference on the management of suicidality in the clinical environment, addressing all of the issues believed essential to establishing minimal competence for day-to-day practice.

TABLE OF CONTENTS

THE ASSESSMENT AND MANAGEMENT OF SUICIDALITY

INTRODUCTION

Suicide risk assessment has become a routine task among clinicians working in outpatient settings. As inpatient alternatives have slowly dwindled and lengths of stay have decreased dramatically over the past two decades (e.g., Rudd et al., 1999), it has become increasingly important that mental health practitioners be well informed about, and comfortable with, assessing suicide risk and managing those at-risk in outpatient settings. There is little doubt that those in clinical practice will see suicidal patients even if they are not identified as working in the specialty area. It is difficult, if not impossible, to so tightly control the patient flow to prevent these individuals from appearing through routine referral channels. Although detailed discussions of the issue are available in the extant literature (e.g., Rudd, Joiner, & Rajab, 2004), I have yet to find a brief, thorough, and easily accessible clinical guide to suicide risk assessment, one that clinicians of all stripes can review in a short time frame.

This book was written to fill that gap in the literature. It is intended to be a book that you can put in your briefcase if moving from one clinical setting to another or lay on your desk and refer to when needed between patients. Accordingly, I will not offer an in-depth theoretical discussion of the multitude of issues in suicidality or a detailed review of the empirical literature. For that, readers are referred to some of my other work (e.g., Rudd et al., 2004). The intent here is to offer an accessible guide to practicing clinicians that will aid day-to-day practice in an easy and efficient fashion; a clinical resource for the novice practitioner, student in training, or seasoned professional. This is a clinical resource that is focused specifically on the assessment and immediate management of suicidality, not ongoing treatment or psychotherapy.

This book has several goals, all directly related to improving the quality of clinical care provided to suicidal patients. First, I want to emphasize the importance of language in clinical practice. We need to be precise in the definitions we use; this includes how we talk to patients, how we talk to one another, and how we document our assessment and management decisions. I truly believe that such precision translates to improved clinical practice, with more accurate suicide risk assessments, greater consistency and continuity over time and across patients, better clinical decision making, and ultimately better clinical care. Second, I want to stress the need for clinicians to adopt a standard framework for suicide risk assessment — one grounded in empirical research and the science of clinical psychology, that can be modified over time as more information becomes available, and that can be applied seamlessly and consistently across all patients in your practice. Third, I want to highlight the need to be predictable, blunt, and straightforward with the suicidal patient, providing a firm foundation and predictable process in the relationship. Fourth, the importance of consistent, clear, and thorough documentation can never be overemphasized. And finally, the importance of accessible, reliable, and well-informed consultation is critical. We all get stuck at times, for different reasons, and need someone ready, willing, and able to provide much-needed consultation and guidance.

I hope you read this guide with the preceding goals in mind, and I hope you find it useful as a pocket guide, something that you will refer to frequently in day-to-day practice. But, given the focus of the book, there will undoubtedly be shortcomings. You may well find yourself wanting more detailed discussion of targeted issues. If so, I refer you on to some of my other work. I have included examples of several forms and documents that you can copy or modify as needed. Those included were developed with two potentially contradictory forces in mind: the need to be thorough and the demands of daily clinical practice. As a practitioner myself, I am fully aware of the significant time constraints faced in the clinical trenches. I have also ended each section with *points to remember for the practitioner* in an effort to highlight those issues I believe most critical to clinical practice with suicidal patients. The *points to remember* offer a succinct summary of critical issues for practice, things you can translate directly into clinical care with suicidal patients. Although assessing and treating suicidality is among the most professionally challenging and anxiety-provoking tasks a clinician faces (Pope & Tabachnick, 1993), it can also be among the most rewarding. Consistent use of a standard framework and clear documentation not only makes the task easier, it improves the quality and nature of care and it leads to clinical decision making that is collaborative and defensible in the unlikely event it is ever legally challenged. In short, it helps save lives.

Hindsight bias is a huge problem in cases of suicide. At least from a forensic perspective, it is almost always argued that it was *foreseeable* that a particular patient was at risk for suicide, particularly because he or she was already engaged in the mental health or health care system and likely presented with multiple markers of risk. When a life is tragically lost to suicide, it is imperative that the clinician be able to provide documentation offering a clear, specific, and succinct rationale for clinical decisions. Trust me, a host of questions will be directed at the practitioner:

- Why was a patient who was thinking about suicide or had made a suicide attempt not hospitalized?
- Why was a given course of treatment followed when there were indications that the patient was not responding well or getting better?
- Did you consider alternative treatment options?
- Was medication considered?
- What did you do to safeguard the patient's environment?
- What steps were taken in response to the identified risk level?
- Did you make an effort to talk with and enlist the help of family?
- Did the patient have a crisis response plan in place to deal with unexpected crises?

These are just a few of the questions that frequently come up in the course of a postsuicide forensic review. Remember the issue of hindsight bias. In cases of suicidality, it is simply easier and clinically more appropriate, efficient, and effective to ask and answer these questions from the beginning. That is really the intent of this book; to help you understand well in advance the notion of "core competencies" or the "standard of care in suicidality." As a practicing clinician, it is important to understand what others expect; what they think qualifies as "competent care." In many respects, each of the topics covered in this book represents an underlying core competency in the assessment and management of suicidality.

It is important to understand that the standard of care is a fluid construct, one defined independently for each claim and case of malpractice or negligence. Ultimately it is defined by the expert witness testifying in court. Nevertheless, there still are common elements, including (a) foreseeability, (b) treatment planning, and (c) follow-up or follow-through (Jobes & Berman, 1993). This book was written with these common elements in mind, particularly the issue of hindsight bias and perceived foreseeability. In many forensic cases, the issue of foreseeability is confused with the issue of predictability. More specifically, as clinicians, many of us believe that we can somehow predict individual suicides. There is ample scientific evidence that low base-rate problems like suicide cannot be meaningfully predicted on an individual basis (cf. Pokorny, 1992). Regardless, the expectation persists, and all practitioners should keep this in mind.

Although we cannot reliably predict individual suicides, we can determine periods of heightened risk, what Litman (1989) referred to as the *suicide zone*. When we have recognized escalating risk, we need to respond accordingly and then continue to monitor the situation and respond in accordance with subsequent clinical markers until risk resolves. If we refer someone out for further evaluation or treatment, we need to follow up and see if the referral was kept. If not, we need to explore why not. If the acute suicidal state continues, then we again need to respond as clinically indicated. In short, this is a clinical application of the three elements of the standard of practice in suicidality: foreseeability, treatment planning, and follow-up. These three elements apply regardless of whether or not we see a patient one time or twenty. It is essential that we complete thorough and accurate risk assessments (foreseeability), respond appropriately (treatment planning), and make sure our plan was implemented (follow-up) even if we are not the one providing the continuing care.

As you work your way through this book, you will recognize these three elements throughout. As an active forensic reviewer, I keep these elements in mind in all aspects of clinical care, regardless of which of the three domains is being targeted. Although this book by no means defines the standard of care in working with suicidal patients, it certainly keeps the critical elements at the forefront. As mentioned before, this book really represents minimal "core competencies" in suicide risk assessment and immediate management. There certainly is a different and more complicated set of core competencies if the target is short- or long-term psychotherapy with suicidal patients. Accordingly, if you are attentive to the content (and related process issues) covered in this text, you will be responsive to what some have referred to as the "core competencies" in suicide risk assessment and immediate management.

TERMINOLOGY:
THE IMPORTANCE OF BEING PRECISE

When a patient dies by suicide, it is painful for everyone involved: the surviving family members and friends, the clinician or clinicians providing care, and the institution involved. Having served for many years now on morbidity/mortality review committees, as well as having consulted in a great many forensic cases, I have noticed that clinicians all too often make a painful situation more complex with case notes that employ imprecise, misleading, and at times simply inaccurate descriptions of a patient's behavior. The definitions of suicide and suicidal behavior would seem to be relatively straightforward — that is, until we look at applying the definitions in a clinical environment. What initially seemed like a simple black-and-white issue very quickly becomes gray and confused. As many who will read this book can attest, there is great disparity in how individual clinicians define suicidal ideation and behavior, much less the degree of precision and specificity offered in documentation.

What exactly do we mean by the term suicidal? Is it a dichotomous construct, or does suicidality exist on a continuum? A number of terms have surfaced in the literature, oftentimes with little or poor clarification. Among them are parasuicidal behavior, self-mutilatory behavior, self-abuse, self-injury, morbid ruminations, self-destructive behavior, and subintentioned death. How do we differentiate these from suicide attempts or completed suicides? The scenarios provided below hint at the possible stumbling blocks presented by simply defining (and describing) patient behavior. Of the following scenarios,* which ones represent suicidal behavior?

---

* Names and identifying characteristics of persons in all case examples have been disguised thoroughly to protect privacy.

- **<u>Scenario 1</u>**: An adolescent girl rushes into the family room where her mother, father, and two younger siblings are watching TV. She loudly proclaims that she *can't stand it anymore since her boyfriend left her and wants to die.* She promptly takes a handful of aspirin.
- **<u>Scenario 2</u>**: A middle-aged woman, feeling depressed and having persistent suicidal thoughts, has not told anyone about her depression. She lives alone and is isolated. One evening, she starts to drink heavily and cuts on her wrist and draws blood. She later stops and goes to bed, simply returning to her daily routine the next morning. She eventually discloses the incident to her family physician, adding *I don't really think I wanted to die.*
- **<u>Scenario 3</u>**: A middle-aged man retreats to an isolated, wooded area out by a lake near his house. He has not told anyone where he was going or that he has been thinking of suicide. He has been depressed since losing his job 2 months prior. He takes out a loaded gun, places it to his head, and, after a few minutes, puts the gun away and returns home to his wife and child, never divulging anything to his family about what happened. He tells his primary care physician 3 weeks later during a routine check-up, at which time he hesitantly acknowledges that he's *been very, very depressed.*
- **<u>Scenario 4</u>**: A young male in his early 20s is at home alone after his parents left for the weekend. He takes a packet of information (including his will, financial records, and letters to his family members), places it under his feet, and hangs himself in the closet. His body is discovered by his parents when they return home.
- **<u>Scenario 5</u>**: An intoxicated young female takes an overdose in her dorm room while her two college roommates are in the next room. Within a few minutes, she walks into the living area, obviously drunk, and tells her roommates that *she took something because she wants her boyfriend to know how much she loves him.* Her friends call 9-1-1 and she is taken to the local emergency room for evaluation but is released within a few hours.
- **<u>Scenario 6</u>**: An adolescent male rushes to the kitchen after a heated argument with his parents. He frantically looks under

the sink and impulsively drinks some bleach as his parents follow right after him. They take him to the local emergency room where he tells the ER physician that he *was just mad* and *really didn't want to die.* He returns home with his parents a few hours after the evaluation.

In the scenarios listed above, what we would consider suicidal depends on a number of factors. As O'Carroll et al. (1996) have noted, suicidal behavior can be distinguished by three characteristic features: intent to die, evidence of self-infliction, and outcome (injury, no injury, or death). In accordance with these features, they have offered the following definitions:

Suicide: Death from injury, poisoning, or suffocation where there is evidence (either implicit or explicit) that the injury was self-inflicted and that the decedent intended to kill himself/herself. Note: the term completed suicide can be used interchangeably with the term suicide.

Suicide Attempt With Injuries: An action resulting in nonfatal injury, poisoning, or suffocation where there is evidence (either implicit or explicit) that the injury was self-inflicted and that he/she intended at some level to kill himself/herself.

Suicide Attempt Without Injuries: A potentially self-injurious behavior with a nonfatal outcome, for which there is evidence (either implicit or explicit) that the person intended at some level to kill himself/ herself.

Instrumental Suicide-Related Behavior: Potentially self-injurious behavior for which there is evidence (either implicit or explicit) that the person did not intend to kill himself/herself (i.e., zero intent to die) and the person wished to use the appearance of intending to kill himself/herself in order to attain some other end (e.g., to seek help, to punish others, or to receive attention). Instrumental suicide-related behavior can occur with injuries, without injuries, or with fatal outcome (i.e., accidental death).

Suicide Threat: Any interpersonal action, verbal or nonverbal, stopping short of a directly self-harmful act that a reasonable person would interpret as communicating or suggesting that a suicidal act or other suicide-related behavior might occur in the near future.

Suicidal Ideation: Any self-reported thoughts of engaging in suicide-related behavior. (pp. 240-241)*

It is critical to take intent, outcome, and self-infliction into consideration before characterizing a behavior as suicidal. It may well be that the behavior was *motivated* by a reason other than death (e.g., Scenarios 2 and 5 above) and has a high *probability for rescue* (e.g., Scenarios 1, 5, and 6); both variables demonstrate the intent behind the behavior. In the cases mentioned (Scenarios 1, 2, 5, and 6), markers of objective intent (see discussion below) suggest that the observed behaviors may well be instrumental (i.e., motivation other than death) in nature rather than specifically suicidal. Accurately differentiating suicidal and instrumental behaviors is important for a number of reasons:

- It improves the consistency and accuracy of the individual clinician's assessments. In other words, the same behavior is described as suicidal across different circumstances and contexts.
- It improves communication between clinicians working with the same individual, as well as between the clinician and patient.
- In cases of chronic suicidality, liability can be reduced by being able to differentiate between episodes of instrumental behavior and periods of acute suicidality. In other words, rather than erroneously documenting that the patient "reported 10 suicide attempts," careful scrutiny and evaluation may reveal two suicide attempts and eight episodes of instrumental suicide-related behavior of low lethality, with clear motivation for something other than death. As will be discussed later, the clinical response to instrumental behavior is, in many ways, different than that for a suicide attempt. As will also be discussed in more detail in a later section, instrumental behavior is consistent with those manifesting chronic suicidality.
- It improves the nature of clinical care, with the clinician responding in appropriate and titrated fashion to each independent situation. Acute suicidal states demand a different response than chronic instrumental states. This is not to say

---

*Note: From "Beyond the Tower of Babel: A nomenclature for suicidology" by P. O'Carroll, A. Berman, R. Maris, E. Moscicki, B. Tanney, and M. Silverman, 1996, *Suicide and Life-Threatening Behavior, 26*, pp. 240-241. Copyright © 1996 by Guilford Publications, Inc. Reprinted with permission.

that accidental death does not occur when people engage in instrumental behavior; it does. Instrumental behavior can indeed result in accidental death, with it being categorized as accidental because the patient was not motivated to die; rather death was a consequence of a high-risk behavior. There is a broad range of high-risk behaviors, some more obviously self-destructive than others (e.g., cutting versus driving at excessive speeds).

When thinking about differentiating among suicide attempts, instrumental behavior, and suicide threats, the critical variable to consider is intent. You can think about intent in two overlapping, but not identical, ways. First, there is subjective or *expressed* intent. This is what the patient says to you. Did the patient say he or she wants (wanted) to kill himself or herself? Be sure to document exactly what the patient said; directly quoting the patient is preferred and recommended (e.g., *I'm going to shoot myself* or *I wish I had died from taking the pills*). Second, there is objective or observed intent. This is essentially what the patient does; that is, concrete behavior you observe. Again, describe the behavior in simple and direct terms. Did the patient prepare for suicide (e.g., write letters to children, parents, a spouse; get financial documents in order; revise a will)? Did he or she take actions to prevent discovery and/or rescue? Was the attempt in an isolated, secluded, or protected area? Was the attempt timed in such a way as to prevent discovery (e.g., when the patient knew no one would be home for hours or days)? Was rescue and intervention only by random chance? Markers of objective intent include behaviors that demonstrate

- a desire to die,
- preparation for death (e.g., letters to loved ones, organizing financial records, obtaining or modifying insurance policies, writing or revising a will), and
- efforts to prevent discovery or rescue.

Obviously, one of the most powerful markers of objective intent is any effort to prevent discovery and/or rescue during an attempt. Patients who deny intent to die but have expended considerable effort to prevent discovery or have taken steps to impede their rescue provide observable, concrete evidence of intent to die. Such evidence needs to be weighed in clinical assessment and decision making. Understanding, observing, and discussing markers of objective intent with patients is a critical part of the assessment process.

More often than not, what the patient says and does will agree. Over the years, I have found patients to be fairly direct and honest in their reports. It is the unusual case where manipulation, deception, or malingering is the question. In some cases, though, there will be discrepancies. Patients will say one thing and do another. They may say they are not suicidal when their behavior suggests something very much to the contrary (e.g., an attempt of high lethality; taking steps to prevent rescue; extensive preparation for death prior to the attempt). Clarifying and resolving such discrepancies is one of the more important tasks in the risk assessment process. Challenging the patient when there is a discrepancy is the only route to effective resolution. For example:

> *You've told me that you really don't want to die, but all of your behavior over the last few weeks suggests otherwise. You've been drinking heavily, you've written a letter to your husband saying you wanted to die, and several weeks ago you took an overdose when you knew no one would be home and waited 3 days to tell me about it. I need for you to help me make some sense of this contradiction. It almost seems like you're telling me one thing and doing another. Frankly, I'm more inclined to consider your behavior as the more important variable here, particularly since I'm very concerned about your safety and well-being.*

When challenged in this way, I can tell you that many patients will routinely acknowledge withholding important information about their intent to die. Seeking such clarification is an effective way to undermine any apparent resistance to an honest and frank exchange about the patient's suicidal thoughts and behaviors, as well as any ambivalence about open and honest reporting. In short, you need to be aware of both subjective and objective markers of intent and resolve any observed discrepancy (any apparent difference between what patients do and what they say). If, during the assessment process, you do not feel that the patient has provided an adequate response to observed intent discrepancies, it is important to remember that there is ample scientific evidence to support disproportionate weighting of the behavior (objective markers of intent) over what the patient says (subjective intent). In short, past suicidal behavior continues to be the best predictor of future suicidal behavior (cf. Joiner et al., 2005). What a patient does, particularly if it is done repeatedly, carries great significance.

POINTS TO REMEMBER FOR THE PRACTITIONER

1. Whether or not you use the terminology offered here, restrict the range of terminology used in your practice. Be sure that everyone in your practice (clinic, unit, etc.) agrees on the definitions of suicide attempt, instrumental behavior, suicide threat, suicide ideation, and related terminology (e.g., morbid ruminations, self-injury, or self-harm).

2. When identifying suicide attempts, always note whether there is any associated injury, that is, a suicide attempt with or without injuries. If there are injuries, you need to note the associated lethality (both actual and that perceived by the patient) and the nature of any medical care provided. If care was needed but not provided, you need to document why not. Did the patient refuse medical care? If so, this is an important variable that needs to be documented; it provides evidence of treatment noncompliance. Maintaining a clear record of treatment noncompliance is important, particularly with refractory cases. Assessing perceived lethality is straightforward and can be accomplished with the question: *Did you think taking the pills* (or other method) *would kill you?*

3. Always differentiate between suicide attempts and instrumental behavior. In order to do so, you must have a clear understanding and assessment of intent. You will need to differentiate subjective from objective intent and reconcile any apparent discrepancies. As is discussed in later sections, this will require you to go through all reported suicide attempts, something that can be very time-consuming and not practical in the initial session.

4. In cases where multiple suicide attempts are reported, explore each and every attempt separately. It is critical to effectively differentiate suicidal and instrumental episodes.

This may well take more than one session for many patients. For those with chronic suicidality, it may take three to five sessions. In a later section I will talk about agreeing to an extended evaluation with the patient. You will find the investment of time and energy to explore each and every attempt extremely valuable. Careful differentiation early in the assessment and treatment process lays a foundation of clarity and honesty with the patient. It can also be argued that the careful use of terminology is, in itself, a clinical intervention. Greater clarity in your communication with a suicidal patient helps both you and the patient understand that, even in cases of chronic suicidality, the patient is not always suicidal. Patients often find great relief in the realization that there are differences between morbid ruminations and self-mutilatory and suicidal thoughts, as well as differences between suicide attempts and instrumental behaviors. Quite frequently I will have patients respond with a comment like, *It's nice to know that I don't always want to die; that I was just looking for relief from my pain.* As is evident in this comment, precision and clarity of communication lays the foundation for subsequent psychotherapy targeting emotion regulation skills, among a host of other issues. In these cases, greater precision in your terminology is actually a clinical intervention.

5. Don't vacillate in the terminology used; consistently refer to either "suicide" or "killing yourself" during the interview. Some of our exit interviews with suicidal patients revealed anecdotal evidence that patients believed clinicians were "nervous and didn't really want to talk" when terminology vacillated greatly during the interview (cf. Rudd et al., 2004). As previously noted, the clear and specific use of terminology will help provide an honest and blunt foundation for the therapeutic relationship, facilitating an accurate report by the patient and thorough understanding on the part of the clinician.

6. Always be precise in your terminology! This includes discussions with patients and between clinicians.

UNDERSTANDING THE
NATURE OF RISK OVER TIME:
DIFFERENTIATING ACUTE AND CHRONIC RISK

Terminology is an essential element of clinical practice. As evidenced in the previous section, it drives how we talk to patients and fellow clinicians about suicidality. And ultimately, it directly impacts the nature of clinical care provided. In some respects, precise terminology and related clarification is a clinical intervention that can be used to reduce patient distress and facilitate a better therapeutic alliance. A sense of control is created when a patient can better describe and differentiate affective/emotional states, particularly when suicide is at issue. Similarly, the importance of how clinicians think about suicidality cannot be overstated, particularly the issue of how we conceptualize suicidality over time. Contrary to what the courts and plaintiff's attorneys would have us believe, suicidality is not a static construct. Once suicidal does not mean always suicidal. Suicidal states come and they go. Simply because a patient has made a suicide attempt does not mean that a subsequent suicide 8 months later was predictable and a direct function of the previous attempt. Intervening events occur and can be (and are) unpredictable. Because a patient is suicidal on Tuesday does not mean he or she will be suicidal on Wednesday. There is certainly more than one response to a suicidal patient; hospitalization is not the only alternative. The variability in response to suicidal patients is due, in part, to the fluid nature of risk over time.

Think back about the essential elements of the standard of care; the issue of foreseeability is a challenging one, particularly in cases of chronic suicide risk or what Maris (1992) referred to as "suicidal careers." Consistent with Litman's (1989) notion of the suicide zone, suicide risk varies over time; periods of heightened risk come and go, even for those individuals who are considered at chronic risk. It is important to have a conceptual model for understanding suicide risk over time; this is essential prior to talking about the content of the assessment. Such a conceptual model helps guide the process of risk assessment with a patient over time, making clinical decisions straightforward even for those with long suicidal histories.

I will address the content of suicide risk assessment later in this book. The current section discusses an approach to conceptualizing the process of risk, that is, how risk changes over time. The goal of this section is to provide a model for understanding the relationship between acute suicidal states and those that endure over longer periods. Before discussing the "what" of suicide risk assessment, it is important to have a conceptual model for thinking about "how" suicidality emerges in the first place, eventually subsides, and reemerges later on, and how it is maintained over time. In short, we need to be able to answer some very basic questions about suicidality:

- How can the clinician understand the relationship between one suicide attempt and subsequent attempts?
- Does one attempt result in increased vulnerability for future attempts or eventual suicide?
- If there is in fact a temporal relationship between attempts, what is the mechanism of action?
- Do patients who make repeated suicide attempts have lower thresholds for becoming suicidal in the first place?
- How long will an episode of suicidality last?
- Are there variables that differentiate short- versus long-duration suicidal crises? In other words, do we know when a crisis will last a long time or might subside quickly?
- How severe will the suicidal episode be, and what is the course of recovery like?
- Do all symptoms remit in unison, or should we expect certain symptoms to resolve before others?
- Resolution of what symptoms lowers suicide risk?

The theory discussed here, fluid vulnerability theory, will answer some of these questions but certainly not all. This theory has been presented in more detail elsewhere (Rudd, 2006). Consistent with the goal of this book, the current discussion is necessarily brief in nature, addressing only the central issue of differentiating acute and chronic risk, rather than the fundamental assumptions of the theory, along with other theoretical implications. The reader is referred to Rudd (2006) for a detailed discussion of the theory, along with supporting empirical work.

Previous research has demonstrated that there are indeed differences among those who think about suicide, those who attempt one time, and those who make multiple suicide attempts (Rudd, Joiner, & Rajab, 1995).

It is undeniable that some suicide ideators will go on to become attempters and that some single attempters will go on to become multiple attempters. It is of critical importance for clinicians to have an understanding of chronic or enduring suicidal risk in an effort to differentiate these populations during the assessment process and make appropriate clinical decisions. Fluid vulnerability theory (FVT; Rudd, 2006) is a way to understand the distinctions among ideators, attempters, and multiple attempters. It is a conceptual model that helps us understand the process of risk over both short- and long-term periods.

According to FVT, all individuals have a baseline level of risk that varies in accordance with personal history and related static factors (e.g., psychiatric diagnosis; treatment history; history of emotional, physical, or sexual abuse). Static factors are personal variables that will not change. For individuals who have made two or more suicide attempts (i.e., multiple attempters), their baseline risk is higher than those who think about suicide or have made single attempts. These have to be genuine suicide attempts, with indications of intent to die. In other words, multiple attempters are simply more vulnerable to experiencing a suicidal crisis relative to all others. It takes less to trigger suicidality in multiple attempters, and, when they become suicidal, they tend to experience more severe symptoms, have more specific suicidal thoughts, express more intent to die, and the symptom constellation tends to last longer. There is convincing and converging evidence now that multiple attempters experience more enduring and severe psychopathology relative to ideators and single attempters, consistent with this notion of lower "thresholds of activation" for a suicidal crisis (Clark & Fawcett, 1992; Forman et al., 2004; Rudd, Joiner, & Rajab, 1996).

FVT emphasizes two primary points: First, multiple attempters are more vulnerable, for any number of reasons, and it takes less to trigger an acute episode of suicidality. Second, suicidal states are time-limited; suicidal intent and associated heightened symptomatology do not last an indeterminate period of time. What is embedded in these two characteristic features of FVT is that suicidal states or crises have both (a) acute (time-limited periods of high or extreme risk secondary to symptom elevation and escalating intent to die) and (b) chronic (enduring vulnerability and heightened susceptibility) features. Although those at chronic risk are at elevated risk day in and day out, it is important to recognize that this is the normative state for these individuals. In accordance with FVT, those with a history of multiple suicide attempts manifest chronic suicidality as well as the more readily recognized acute features during a crisis state. In short, the clinician should be aware that when a patient has a history of multiple suicide attempts, the clinician will need to talk about chronic risk in his or her write-up. Even though acute symptoms and intent have subsided, the patient's heightened susceptibility to future suicidal crises has not. This needs to be acknowledged in the chart. If it is not specifically stated that the patient poses a chronic risk for suicide, then the implicit (and wrong) assumption is that that the patient is not at risk once the acute crisis (i.e., acute symptoms) has resolved. Acknowledging chronic risk for a patient indicates that the threshold for intensive care and intervention for this patient is different than for others. It recognizes that these individuals have enduring vulnerabilities that cannot be effectively treated by inpatient or other acute care alternatives. Such enduring vulnerabilities are only effectively treated over longer periods of time.

Translating FVT into practical application in the clinical environment is straightforward. What triggers (precipitates) a suicidal state, the specificity of ideation and associated intent, accompanying symptoms, and the duration of the crisis are all time-limited phenomena. These are all acute aspects of the suicidal state. In contrast, the patient's susceptibility to becoming suicidal in the first place (i.e., suicidal threshold), his or her inherent ability to take steps to manage and resolve the crisis, and the potential for future episodes are all a function of more enduring individual characteristics, traits, and experiences. These are all enduring or chronic aspects of the suicidal state that need to be recognized and discussed by the clinician, but all too often go neglected in clinical write-ups. Current scientific evidence supports identifying multiple attempters as particularly unique in this respect (cf. Forman et al., 2004; Rudd et al., 1996). In my more detailed discussion of FVT (Rudd, 2006), I identified that individual susceptibility extends across several identifiable domains: cognitive susceptibility (impaired problem solving; lack of cognitive flexibility/cognitive rigidity; cognitive distortions in thinking), biological susceptibility (physiological and affective symptom sensitivity and ceiling), and behavioral susceptibility (deficient skills such as problems in interpersonal interactions and impaired self-soothing and emotion regulation ability).

In short, a thorough assessment of suicide risk demands that the clinician address both acute and chronic features of the patient's suicidality. Identifying these features is fairly simple. In the following sections I will go into detail about assessing suicidal thoughts and related risk factors, along with how to distill that information in risk formulation and response. For now, we will focus on making the distinction between acute and chronic aspects of the patient's suicidality. Acute elements include the nature of suicidal thinking, associated intent, and symptoms (e.g., depression, anxiety, agitation, impulsivity). The distinctive feature of acute elements is that all vacillate in severity and will remit, at least to some degree, as the suicidal crisis resolves. Variations in severity of acute elements of a suicidal state can fluctuate significantly from minute to minute, across the span of a few hours, to days and weeks.

In contrast, chronic features are static and include the patient's susceptibility to becoming suicidal in the first place (i.e., suicidal threshold), which is a function of his or her inherent ability to take steps to manage and resolve the crisis. Current empirical evidence points to a single variable as evidence of chronic suicidality: a history of multiple suicide attempts. Although a history of multiple suicide attempts will invariably be a part of a patient's history, it is possible for chronic features to improve and eventually resolve. However, this only happens after effective long-term care. Perhaps the simplest way to think about chronic features of suicidality is to conceptualize them as enduring maladaptive personality traits consistent with Axis II psychopathology. The traits, coping, and cognitive styles that provide the foundation for Axis II psychopathology can only be altered with long-term care. An acknowledgment of the presence of chronic features to a patient's suicide risk is an acknowledgment of the importance of personality structure and individual choice in driving human behavior, particularly self-destructive behavior. In short, an acknowledgment of chronic aspects to the patient's suicidality is an acknowledgment that foreseeability is relative; that is, we certainly know that someone is vulnerable for crises, but knowing when an acute crisis will emerge is simply impossible.

Points to Remember for the Practitioner

1. All suicidal states have acute and chronic elements. It is important for the clinician to differentiate the two conceptually and practically.

2. Acute elements include the nature of suicidal thinking, associated intent, and symptomatology (e.g., depression, anxiety, agitation, impulsivity). Chronic features include the patient's susceptibility to becoming suicidal in the first place (i.e., suicidal threshold), his or her inherent ability to take steps to manage and resolve the crisis, and the potential for future episodes. Such enduring risk is indicated by a history of multiple suicide attempts.

3. Multiple suicide attempts need to be confirmed through careful exploration of each reported incident (see pp. 26-34); do not simply "take the patient's word" regarding number of attempts.

4. Multiple suicide attempters manifest chronic suicide risk, in contrast to ideators and single attempters. This does not mean that some ideators and single attempters will not go on to become multiple attempters; it only acknowledges the *current* nature of risk.

5. Risk assessment write-ups need to differentiate between acute and chronic factors for each suicidal episode. In other words, a statement will need to be made about a multiple attempter's ongoing risk even when an acute suicidal state has effectively resolved. The clinician will need to discuss enduring features of a patient's risk, that is, ongoing susceptibility. This includes personality, coping, and cognitive styles.

6. Acute risk will demand immediate clinical attention, whereas chronic risk can be effectively addressed only through continuing long-term care. In some cases, clinicians will need to discuss why long-term care is not possible for such patients. This is most often the case when a patient has inadequate insurance and related financial resources to support long-term psychotherapy and/or medications. As will be discussed again later, a referral to a low-cost provider is necessary.

7. Chronic risk is the day-to-day "expected" risk level for the patient and can be safely and effectively treated in outpatient settings as long as there is not expressed or observed intent to die (Rudd et al., 1996).

TASK NUMBER ONE: ESTABLISHING AND MAINTAINING A RELATIONSHIP

Now that we have a solid conceptual foundation for talking and thinking about suicidality, we will move on to address the more recognizable clinical elements of risk assessment and immediate management. The importance of establishing a strong relationship with the suicidal patient cannot be overstated. Even the best therapeutic techniques are of little value when an adequate relationship has not been formed with the patient. The literature is replete with discussions of this issue (see, e.g., Bongar, 1991, 1992; Jobes, 2000; Jobes & Maltsberger, 1995; Linehan, 1993; Rudd et al., 2004). The importance of the therapeutic relationship in psychotherapy treatment outcome is also well cited (cf. Gaston et al., 1998). Bongar et al. (1989) emphasized that the quality of the therapeutic relationship is one of the most important factors in assessing risk and managing suicidal patients. Similarly, others have stressed that a solid therapeutic relationship is essential to successful assessment and management of suicidal patients (cf. Maltsberger, 1986; Shneidman, 1981, 1984).

More often than not, the extent and accuracy of the clinical assessment will be a function of therapeutic comfort and trust. Motto (1979) referred to "active relatedness" to describe clinician behavior that facilitated a stable attachment and positive alliance with the patient. In particular, he emphasized availability as the central issue, that is, emergency availability, returning phone calls, and scheduling more frequent appointments when necessary. Going a step further, Shneidman (1981, 1984) suggested that it is sometimes necessary for the clinician to foster dependency in order to ensure a strong initial attachment. Perhaps best known, though, for her discussion of relationship issues in the treatment of suicidal patients is Marsha Linehan (1993). She identified three strategies for approaching the relationship with a suicidal patient, all geared toward an ongoing and longer term relationship with the patient. It is important to differentiate the relationship during the initial evaluation process from that of short- and long-term therapy. Although there clearly are similar issues, there are also many that are unique to short- and long-term psychotherapy. Consistent with the goals of the book, we will focus only on the relationship during the initial evaluation process and immediate postevaluation management.

Of particular relevance to the initial evaluation process is general clinician behavior and potential reactions to suicidal patients in general. In particular, Maltsberger and Buie (1974, 1989) have referred to "countertransference hate" as a notably malignant reaction, similar to Linehan's (1993) "therapy interfering behaviors." Both include emotional reactions and behaviors such as fear, malice, aversion, hate, anxiety, worry, ending sessions early, taking phone calls during session, being late for appointments, and rescheduling appointments. In short, it is critical for the clinician to explore and address personal beliefs and history relevant to suicidality prior to assessing and working with suicidal patients.

The clinician needs to identify potentially problematic personal beliefs and professional responsibilities prior to engaging suicidal patients. The following questions can help in the process:

- **Why Do People Kill Themselves?** This question will help you articulate your personal theory of suicide. What is important about your personal theory is that it identifies things you personally believe are critical to suicidality. Accordingly, you are likely to ask questions about these areas and explore them in depth, potentially neglecting other critical domains. What is important is that any theory of suicidality be grounded in empirical science. We should all ask questions and pursue information that has an empirical foundation. If you discover that much of what you ask is driven by anecdotal evidence, it may well be a sign that personal beliefs are playing a prominent role.

- **Is It Ever Acceptable to Commit Suicide?** Do you believe that suicide is acceptable in cases of terminal illness? Are there other conditions under which suicide is seen as acceptable? The importance of this question cannot be overstated. It is not uncommon for those suffering medical illness to consider suicide. A clinician's providing implicit or explicit sanction is a particularly risky move for patients seeking care. Regardless of one's position about the issue, it is vital that you explore and identify your personal stance ahead of time. It is also vital that the clinician separate personal belief from professional obligation. Professional obligations with suicidal patients are clear and straightforward. Recognizing, understanding, and distancing potentially problematic personal beliefs ahead of time is crucial.

- **Can Suicide Be Prevented?** This question is important at many different levels. It hints at the clinician's hopefulness, something that is often evident to patients. Feeling overwhelmed and overworked can manifest itself in negative beliefs and attitudes about a patient's potential for recovery. This question also helps identify the clinician's sense of responsibility in terms of intervention and management. What exactly has to be done to prevent suicide?

- **Do People Who Access Care Want to Die?** It is important for all clinicians to explore their thoughts about those accessing care. Why do those expressing hopelessness access care? Accessing care is, in and of itself, an act of hope, even when those presenting are experiencing the most desperate of circumstances. It is important for the clinician to recognize the significance of the simple act of accessing care and reflect this back to the patient. Even in cases of persistent and chronic suicidality, continuing to access care is evidence of hope.

- **What Are Your Individual Professional Responsibilities With a Suicidal Patient?** Your answer to this question will help you articulate the steps you will take in intervention and management following the evaluation process. It is critical to understand that your responsibilities are not endless; rather they should be driven by clearly articulated policies and procedures. If you cannot answer this question in simple and straightforward terms, you likely do not have clarity with regard to existing policies and procedures concerning high-risk patients. This book should help clarify your responsibilities.

The answers to the previous questions will, in many respects, be a function of your personal and professional experience with suicidality. Sorting out your personal stance prior to working with suicidal patients is important. What should drive your behavior with suicidal patients is your professional obligations, not personal history and related emotion. Recognize the potential hurdles presented in these questions and explore them prior to offering clinical care.

Establishing and maintaining a relationship in cases of suicidality is often simplified by the crisis nature of the initial presentation. From the very first contact, the clinician needs to be aware of the patient's level of comfort. As we have demonstrated elsewhere, suicidal patients withdraw prematurely from evaluations and treatment not because of improvement in symptoms but because of severe psychopathology and related interpersonal dysfunction (Rudd et al., 1995). In other words, they often simply cannot tolerate the distress and upset created by the interpersonal contact. Establishing a relationship in the initial evaluation with a suicidal patient can be hampered by the severe nature of the psychopathology presented. It is important to keep the following in mind:

- The patients you see are likely to have difficulty in interpersonal situations. More specifically, it is likely that they have interpersonal skill deficits. They might well have trouble expressing or controlling emotional affect. Accordingly, they might initially be withdrawn or may well be hostile, angry, and explosive. Your goal is to create a safe environment. This can be accomplished by giving them time to talk and reinforcing them even when it is anger and hostility that emerge. Reinforcing interaction and openness on the part of the patient can be straightforward and simple. For example: *I know it's difficult to talk about such personal issues, particularly with someone you've just met. It takes a lot of personal courage to do so.* Similarly, anger and hostility can be handled in a compassionate and understanding manner. For example: *It sounds like you've had a very difficult time over the last few weeks. I certainly understand your upset and anger.*

- Remember the patients you are seeing are likely at their worst because they are actively suicidal. Expect your patients to have trouble with communication. Expect your patients to need reassurance and comfort. It is important for the clinician to recognize that patients in acute suicidal crisis feel powerless and out of control already. They need to be reassured to some degree before an accurate assessment can be achieved. For example: *Is there anything I can do to help you feel more comfortable and make it easier for you to talk? If you need to just take a few minutes to catch your breath you can do that. Sometimes it's easier to talk after you've had a few minutes to relax.*

- Anticipate the possibility of being provoked by suicidal patients. For those with chronic suicidal problems, provocative and undercontrolled behavior is oftentimes routine. Responding to provocation is straightforward. Acknowledge the patient's upset in the context of the current crisis and redirect the patient to the task at hand, emphasizing the collaborative nature of the evaluation process. For example: *I can understand why you'd be so upset. You've had some very painful things happen in the last several weeks. We can take a few minutes and talk more about your marriage if you'd like, but in the next 5 or 10 minutes I'm going to need to ask you some questions and get some information so that we can make a decision about how to respond today and over the next several days.*

- Recognize that in completing the initial assessment process you are laying the groundwork for ongoing care, regardless of whether or not that care is provided by you. Evaluations and assessments are psychotherapeutic exchanges; there is simply no way around this reality. The patient's willingness to continue in treatment and ongoing care is often a function of the initial evaluation. Patients who have a negative experience in the initial evaluation will be more difficult to engage during the next crisis.

POINTS TO REMEMBER FOR THE PRACTITIONER

---

1. Conceptualize the therapeutic relationship and alliance as part of the assessment and management process. As mentioned previously, accurate assessment requires honest and blunt reporting on the part of the patient. It is not just knowing what to ask, but asking it in the context of a relationship founded on trust. Recognize, understand, and respond to this demand from the beginning. Relationship and process issues should always be considered as important as content in a suicide risk assessment. This can frequently be accomplished by setting the tone of the interview with a simple statement such as: *I realize what a difficult time this is for you and that it might not be easy to talk. It's important that you feel comfortable so we can fully and accurately understand the extent of the problems*

you've been struggling with, so please let me know if there's anything in particular I can do to help you feel at ease.

2. Use clear, unambiguous language. Do not leave any room for misinterpretation when talking about the issue of suicide. For example: *You said you've been having thoughts of killing yourself. What exactly have you been thinking? When did you first have thoughts of suicide?*

3. Maintain good eye contact when asking difficult questions. Patients understand the subtleties of interpersonal exchanges, such as markers of discomfort and impatience. The lack of eye contact is an easy one to recognize.

4. From time to time, provide historical and developmental context for the current relationship. The most effective way to do this is to draw parallels between the patient's developmental history, recurrent interpersonal problems, and how these patterns might emerge in the therapeutic relationship. It is important to do this from the very beginning. By emphasizing it, you will make it acceptable and expected that the patient voice these problems and actively discuss them should treatment continue after the initial assessment. Not only should it be acceptable to talk about relationship problems in treatment, it should be actively encouraged and reinforced. For example: *We discussed a number of relationship problems that you have had over the years, and I don't believe it'd be inaccurate to say that those problems have been repeated, and it sounds like the same problems have emerged even in therapy relationships in the past. Let me give you an example. You said that you always felt criticized and rejected by your father and that ever since that time the problem surfaces in close relationships, particularly with men. So it wouldn't be surprising if you didn't feel entirely comfortable with me asking detailed and specific questions about your life. Given some of the experiences in your life, it makes perfect sense. If you start to feel that way today, just let me know. We'll talk about it and see if there's anything we can do to make it easier for you. It's important that you and I both come to a good understanding of why you've been thinking about suicide so we can take appropriate steps to help you.*

5. When the opportunity emerges, ask specific questions about problems the patient has had during previous treatment. More than likely this will not happen in the first session. Such issues do not routinely emerge until after three or four sessions. Regardless, though, it is important to know exactly what kinds of interpersonal problems the patient has experienced in previous treatment efforts. Most likely, those with chronic suicidality will have had many experiences in the mental health system. You need to know what to look for and what areas might be particularly sensitive. If so, you might be able to anticipate problems. The patient can provide concrete examples that will facilitate discussion of the therapeutic relationship and, simultaneously, facilitate the current relationship. This will also give you some gauge for the patient's degree of insight and understanding of relationship dynamics. For example, later in the assessment process, the following would be appropriate: *Given some of the problems we've discussed about close relationships, I was wondering if you ran into any of these problems with your previous therapist(s)? How did you handle them? What made it easier for you to deal with it (them)? What made it more difficult? Did you just stop going? What kind of an impact did this have on you? Did you start feeling hopeless about whether treatment can help?*

6. Make the therapy relationship a routine and consistent item on the treatment agenda if the patient continues beyond the initial evaluation (e.g., designate a few minutes at the end of every other session to talk about it). It is important to place the therapeutic relationship in proper perspective. For example: *I'm glad we've had the opportunity to discuss the therapy relationship in a little more detail. It's my thought that this needs to be done on a regular basis, maybe every couple of weeks or once a month, or whenever the circumstances demand it. It's important that you feel comfortable enough to bring up your concerns. I know this won't be easy, especially early on. Please let me know if there's anything I can do to make this process easier for you. What are your thoughts and feelings about what I've said so far?*

Clearly, the therapeutic relationship needs to be addressed in a consistent manner from the initial evaluation throughout the course of immediate follow-up. This book is purposefully focused on the initial evaluation process, not ongoing treatment of suicidal patients. Accordingly, the full range of interpersonal issues in therapy is neither explored nor addressed.

ASSESSING SUICIDAL THINKING AND BEHAVIORS: THE IMPORTANCE OF BEING SPECIFIC

As has been emphasized throughout this brief guide, the need to be precise in suicide risk assessment is critical. This is particularly true when assessing suicidal thoughts. In conducting forensic reviews, I frequently encounter charts that simply indicate that a patient "is thinking about suicide" or "not thinking about suicide," without a detailed discussion of the related parameters. Oftentimes, I see the same thing in terms of notations about a previous history of suicidal behavior or an unspecified attempt. All too often there are no notations about the specifics of an attempt, whether there was any injury associated with the attempt, and whether medical care was indicated or pursued. In the absence of details, retrospective interpretation of entries can be problematic.

There are significant risks in making simple and brief notations without offering clarifying details, with the most probable being that an assessment characterized by vagueness and imprecision will be interpreted as one indicative of high risk. After all, the only time that this issue will be actively debated by clinicians and others involved (such as morbidity and mortality committees) is when there is a bad outcome in the case — either a suicide attempt with serious injury or a suicide. Under these circumstances, it is likely that a suit has already been filed and the chart is under expert review. Accordingly, each and every time suicidal ideation or behavior is mentioned in the chart, it will be assumed that the ideation was specific, enduring, and severe with associated intent to die given that the patient died by suicide. This implies enduring and unresolved risk and, accordingly, lays the foundation for negligence on the part of the provider. Hindsight bias in these cases is a tremendous problem. Often the most trivial aspect of the case is reinterpreted from the myopic lens that the patient was obviously at risk because he or she died (remember the issue of foreseeability?). Detailed evaluation and documentation is an easy (and not too time-consuming) solution to the problem. It is simply unnecessary for a clinician to inadvertently elevate his or her own liability through careless evaluation and documentation practices. A thorough evaluation of suicidal thinking can be accomplished in a fairly brief period of time. It is important for the reader to remember the issues discussed in earlier sections regarding intent along with differentiating acute and chronic risk. It is also important to remember that a common framework should be used for all patients. Asking about suicide takes just a few seconds. And asking about the details of any apparent suicidal thinking takes only a few minutes more.

Figure 1 (p. 28) provides a flow chart of questions that need to be asked of the suicidal patient in order to clarify the nature and severity of his or her suicidal thinking. The critical question is *Have you had thoughts about suicide?* As mentioned before, it is important to use unambiguous language. It is also important to differentiate between morbid ruminations (i.e., thoughts about death, dying, and not wanting to be alive) and suicidal thoughts (thoughts of killing oneself). The two are differentiated by an active desire to kill oneself, not mere passive thoughts of being dead. Some have referred to morbid ruminations as passive suicidal thoughts (cf. Maris et al., 1992), but I find the term morbid ruminations easier for patients to understand. It clearly distinguishes the term from suicidal and is more consistent with the general construct of depression.

Many depressed patients will report morbid ruminations. It is important to help them understand the difference from the very beginning. As noted previously, this leads to a much more accurate risk assessment process in the future when the patient can clearly identify his or her own suicidality. You can also work to normalize the thoughts within the context of an active depressive problem — an intervention that often helps reduce anxiety, agitation, and associated dysphoria. For example, the following statement can be used to normalize morbid thoughts: *It's not unusual for someone who is depressed to feel hopeless and have thoughts about death or dying.* When making the distinction between morbid and suicidal thoughts, it is important to understand that a detailed exploration of the patient's suicidal history still needs to be completed even when the patient does not endorse active suicidal thoughts. If he or she does not have an extensive history, it should take only a few minutes.

FIGURE 1: Exploring Suicidal Thoughts and Getting an Accurate Report

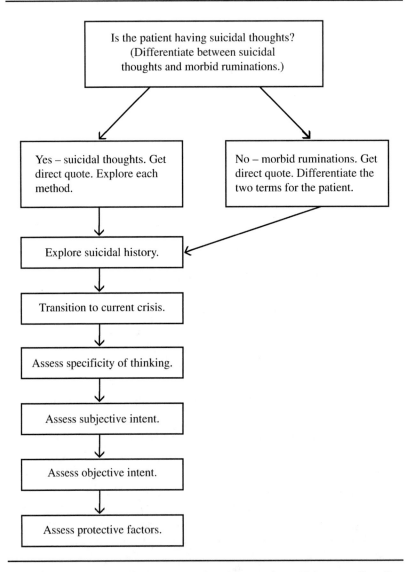

It is best to take direct quotes from the patient. For example: *Can you tell me exactly what you've been thinking?* Taking direct quotes at the beginning of the interview, without providing prompts, provides a means to assess the specificity of the patient's thinking. The specificity of the ideation is one marker of intent, with greater detail and specificity suggesting greater intent. Specificity is captured in the how, when, where, and why of the suicidal crisis. Prior to exploring the details of the current suicidal crisis, it is important to take a strategic step in an effort to reduce any anxiety and resistance associated with the patient's crisis.

After a patient reveals active suicidal thoughts (or, in some cases, morbid ruminations), resistance can be lowered by moving away from the current crisis and briefly exploring the patient's history of suicidality. This can be accomplished with a simple statement: *Before we go into detail about what's going on now, can you tell me about the first time you ever thought about suicide?* If the patient endorses previous suicidal crises, including suicide attempts, it is important to explore each and every one in detail. However, it is unlikely that you can do that in the first interview. Address as many as is reasonable given time constraints and then return to the others in follow-up sessions. For those with chronic suicidal problems it is possible that you might need to agree to an extended evaluation in order to fully assess and understand the patient's history. We will talk more about this later. Among the details that need to be gathered for each previous episode of suicidality are the following contextual factors (the acronym P-N-O-R is useful):

- **<u>Precipitant.</u>** What triggered the crisis, according to the patient? *What triggered your thinking about suicide? Why did you think about killing yourself at the time? Why did you think suicide was the best option at that time in your life?*
- **<u>Nature of Ideation or Attempt.</u>** What was the patient thinking at the time? *To the best of your recollection, can you tell me what you were thinking at the time?* Did he or she want to die? *Did you want to die when you [method]?* What did he or she actually do? *Please tell me exactly what you did.*
- **<u>Outcome.</u>** Was there any associated injury? If so, was medical care required? If required, did the patient follow-through and get care? *Were you injured by the suicide attempt? Did you receive medical care? Why did you choose not to get medical care when it was required?* How did the patient end up accessing care? Was it initiated by the patient? Was it by random chance? *How did you get to the hospital? Did you call someone?* Did

the patient take active steps to prevent discovery or rescue? *Did you take steps to try to prevent your discovery or rescue when you made the suicide attempt? Did you time the attempt or otherwise make it difficult for someone to find you?*

- **Reaction.** What was the patient's reaction to surviving the suicide attempt? *How do you feel about surviving? Did you learn anything helpful about yourself or others from the previous attempt?* What was the patient's perception of the lethality of his or her behavior? *Did you think that [method] would kill you?*

The information gathered above will help you assess both subjective and objective markers of intent. The information will also provide a means to assess the similarity across more than one reported suicidal crisis. Oftentimes, there is similarity in the precipitant and specific details across multiple episodes of suicidality. Sometimes there are indications of escalating lethality and intent to die, a trend that is important to recognize and discuss with the patient. The evolution of intent for a patient, from the perspective of both subjective (whether or not the patient thought the method was lethal) and objective (medical) lethality is critical to recognize and integrate into clinical decision making. If there is a trend of escalating lethality, it will be apparent across episodes. Time constraints are usually paramount in initial evaluations. Accordingly, it is incumbent on the clinician to accurately gauge time and defer detailed exploration of some previous crises or suicide attempts to later sessions if necessary.

Sometimes it will be necessary to complete an extended evaluation of four to five sessions in order to fully understand a patient's suicidal history. If you do not have time for such an extensive evaluation, it is important to make note of that in the chart, deferring the historical review to the next clinician, but clearly indicating that such an extensive review has not yet been accomplished.

After you have explored the patient's suicidal history (either in full or truncated fashion), you can transition back to the current crisis. This can be done in any number of ways. One route is to transition from the first episode of suicidality to the past year, the past month, and then the current episode. If there are a significant number of prior suicide attempts, you can return to explore those as a part of the extended evaluation. In terms of actual questions, it would sound something like this:

- *Can you tell me about the first time you ever thought about suicide [or attempted suicide]?*
- *Have you thought about or attempted suicide in the past year?*
- *Have you thought about or attempted suicide in the past month?*
- *Now let's talk in more detail about the suicidal thoughts that brought you here today.*

Once you have transitioned to the current episode, you need to assess the specificity of the patient's thinking. This includes the frequency, intensity, and duration of thoughts, along with questions about when and where, along with access to the stated method(s). As has been mentioned before, do not provide the patient options to choose from when questioning about method. One indicator of intent is the specificity of the patient's thinking. Prompts can undermine an accurate assessment. They can also lead to a unilateral and unbalanced exchange that can undermine the development of a solid therapeutic relationship. Using the patient's own words (i.e., quoting the patient directly about suicidal thoughts) conveys that you will, and are, listening. It is also important to emphasize the need to question about multiple methods (see below). You need to continue to ask the patient about possible methods and access until he or she says *No, no other methods have been considered.* Patients will sometimes withhold their accessible method until questioned more thoroughly. The meaning embedded in the process of asking about multiple methods is that you care about the patient and you are going to be thorough and specific in the evaluation process. This is yet another example of how detailed inquiry helps build trust and a stronger therapeutic alliance. Specific details about a patient's suicidal thinking can be captured with the following questions:

- *How are you thinking about killing yourself?*
- *Do you have access to [method]?*
- *Have you made arrangements or planned to get access to [method]?*
- *Have you thought about any other way to kill yourself?* Ask this question until the patient says that no other methods have been considered.
- *How often do you think about killing yourself? Once a day, more than once a day, once a week, monthly?*

- *You said you think about suicide every day. How many times a day?*
- *When you have these thoughts, how long do they last? A few seconds, minutes, or longer?*
- *What exactly do you think about for that [period of time]?*
- *When you have these thoughts, how intense or severe are they? Can you rate them on a scale of 1 to 10, with 1 being "not severe at all" and 10 being "so severe that I will act on them"?*
- *Have you thought about when you would kill yourself?*
- *Have you thought about where you would kill yourself?*
- *Have you thought about taking steps or timing your attempt to prevent anyone from finding or stopping you?*

Assessing suicidal thinking in such great detail provides a means not only to assess risk but also to track progress across sessions. It is entirely possible for a patient to improve and evidence little acute or chronic risk despite continuing to think about suicide with some regularity. With chronic suicidality in particular, simple notations in the chart about the presence or absence of suicidal thoughts belie the complexity of the problem. It may well be that a patient has been experiencing suicidal thoughts for decades. The patient could continue to ideate daily but actually be making considerable progress and evidencing no significant risk if the duration (and associated specificity) of the thoughts reduced from, say, 2 hours a day to less than 5 minutes. Reduced duration frequently translates to reduced specificity, less severity, and lower intent, along with lower risk. This frequently parallels a drop in other associated symptoms as well. It is important to recognize that frequency, specificity, intent, and intensity are often interrelated. Simply tracking the daily, weekly, or monthly time allocated to suicidal thinking can be incredibly useful for the practicing clinician. As with any repetitive thought, the acronym F-I-D-S (Frequency-Intensity-Duration-Specificity) helps in prompting the need for the inquiry.

After having queried about the specifics of the patient's suicidal thoughts, you can transition to assessing intent, including both subjective and objective markers. The following questions provide a straight-forward approach to assessing intent:

- *Why do you want to die? What are your reasons for dying?*

- *Do you have any intention of acting on your thoughts? Can you rate your intent on a scale of 1 to 10, with 1 being "no intent at all" and 10 being "certain that you'll act on them as quickly as you can"?*
- *Have you done anything in preparation for your death? Have you taken any steps in preparation (e.g., will, letters to loved ones, rearranged financial records) for death?*
- *Have you rehearsed your suicide in any way? In other words, have you gotten [item for killing yourself] out and gone through the steps to kill yourself?*

The final area relevant to the specifics of suicidal thinking is protective factors. It is important for the clinician to have a clear understanding of what protective factors are in place for the patient — those that are available and accessible during periods of acute crisis. Most important among protective factors are social support and an active treatment relationship (cf. Rudd et al., 2004). Protective factors can be captured with the following questions:

- *Even though you've had a very difficult time, something has kept you going. What are your reasons for living?*
- *Are you hopeful about the future?*
- *What would need to happen to help you be more hopeful about the future?*
- *What keeps you going in difficult times like this?*
- *Whom do you rely on during difficult times?*
- *Has treatment been effective for you in the past?*

Although some of the questions may appear overly detailed, harsh, and blunt, such a specific approach does not result in increased dysphoria and can actually reduce risk (cf. Bender, 2005; Gould et al., 2005). Such detailed questioning helps set the tone and expectations for all subsequent clinical interactions with the patient. It provides an implicit sanction, approval, and reinforcement for the patient being honest and specific with the clinician. Detailed questioning is actually an intervention that facilitates a good therapeutic alliance. Most importantly, though, such an approach provides the details necessary to make accurate risk assessment decisions. In later sections I will review documentation, along with a possible brief format for risk assessment write-ups. Regardless, though, an accurate risk assessment is only possible if accurate patient information is available. This starts with a thorough and detailed understanding of the patient's suicidal thinking.

POINTS TO REMEMBER FOR THE PRACTITIONER

1. When talking about suicide, be specific. Use the term suicide. Do not waffle in your language with the patient. As mentioned in the previous section, a solid therapeutic alliance is critical to an accurate assessment. Precision and specificity in language helps establish just such a relationship. Patients will realize that you will not shy away from painful details and that you truly want to hear everything.

2. Ask for details about suicidal thinking, including what, how, when, where, and why. When talking about suicidal thoughts, be sure to ask about and track the frequency, intensity, duration, and specifity of thoughts. Those with persistent suicidal thoughts, particularly those struggling with chronic suicidality, may well be making progress but that fact will be lost because the characteristic features of the ideations were neglected.

3. Always ask about multiple methods. It is not uncommon for patients to consider multiple methods. Patients sometimes withhold the method with access to see if the clinician will be persistent and thorough. As with the issue of asking about the specifics of the ideations, asking about multiple methods sends an implicit and explicit message to the patient — that you care and that you will be thorough in your approach.

4. Ask about suicidal history before asking about the current crisis; this will reduce anxiety and natural resistance. You can start with the patient's first suicide attempt. If there are multiple attempts, you can transition from the first one to any in the past year, the past month, and then to the current crisis.

5. Be sure to assess both objective and subjective intent related to each suicidal episode.
6. Consider conducting an extended evaluation with those reporting a significant number of prior suicide attempts. Many patients with chronic suicidal problems will simply have too extensive a history to cover in one session. An extended evaluation of four to five sessions provides a means to complete a thorough evaluation prior to making definitive decisions about treatment.

COMPLETING THE PICTURE: ASSESSING OTHER RISK FACTORS

In the previous section I reviewed a detailed assessment of suicidal thinking. This needs to be supplemented with an assessment of additional risk factors, all embedded within a common framework for clinical decision making. The focus here is on the clinical interview, not supplemental psychological testing. A review of psychological assessment instruments is well beyond the scope of this book and is available elsewhere (e.g., Brown, 2001; Goldston, 2003). A critical assumption is that a complete and comprehensive intake history and diagnostic interview will always be conducted as a part of psychiatric and psychological evaluations.

In addition to a detailed and thorough assessment of suicidal thinking, there are a number of empirically supported domains essential to accurately assessing suicide risk (Rudd et al., 2004). As detailed in Table 1 (pp. 36-37), the domains I recommend include identifiable precipitants, the patient's symptomatic presentation, presence of hopelessness, nature of suicidal thinking, previous suicidal behavior, impulsivity and self-control, and protective factors. Although by no means exhaustive, the current domains are those that have good empirical support.

Perhaps the easiest approach to assessing each of the specific domains is to move in hierarchical fashion from the precipitating event, to the patient's current symptom presentation, to hopelessness, to active suicidal thinking. Anxiety and resistance can be reduced by exploring the patient's suicidal history before asking detailed questions about the

TABLE 1: Additional Areas of Risk Assessment

I: Predisposition to Suicidal Behavior

- Previous history of psychiatric diagnoses (increased risk with recurrent disorders, comorbidity, and chronicity) including major depressive disorder, bipolar disorder, schizophrenia, substance abuse, and personality disorders such as borderline personality disorder.
- Previous history of suicidal behavior (increased risk with previous attempts, high lethality, and chronic disturbance). Those having made multiple attempts (i.e., two or more) are considered at chronic risk.
- Recent discharge from inpatient psychiatric treatment (increased risk within first year of release). Risk is highest during the first month postdischarge.
- Same-sex sexual orientation (increased risk among homosexual men)
- Male gender
- History of abuse (sexual, physical, or emotional)
- Age over 60
- Family history of suicide

II: Identifiable Precipitant or Stressors (most can be conceptualized as losses)

- Significant loss (e.g., financial, interpersonal relationships, professional, identity)
- Acute or chronic health problems (can be loss of independence, autonomy, or function)
- Relationship instability (loss of meaningful relationships and related support and resources)

III: Symptomatic Presentation (have patient rate severity on 1-10 scale)

- Depressive symptoms — for example, anhedonia, low self-esteem, sadness, dyssomnia, fatigue (increased risk when combined with anxiety and substance abuse)
- Bipolar disorder (increased risk early in disorder's course)
- Anxiety (increased risk with trait anxiety)
- Schizophrenia (increased risk following active phases)
- Borderline and antisocial personality features

IV: Presence of Hopelessness (have patient rate severity on 1-10 scale)

- Severity of hopelessness
- Duration of hopelessness

V: The Nature of Suicidal Thinking

- Current ideation frequency, intensity, and duration
- Presence of suicidal plan (increased risk with specificity)
- Availability of means
- Lethality of means

- Active suicidal behaviors
- Explicit suicidal intent

VI: Previous Suicidal Behavior

- Frequency and context of previous suicidal behaviors
- Perceived lethality and outcome
- Opportunity for rescue and help-seeking
- Preparatory behaviors

VII: Impulsivity and Self-Control (have patient rate on 1-10 scale)

- Subjective self-control
- Objective control (e.g., substance abuse, impulsive behaviors, aggression)

VIII: Protective Factors

- Presence of social support. Support needs to be both present and accessible. Make sure the relationships are healthy.
- Problem-solving skills and history of coping skills
- Active participation in treatment
- Presence of hopefulness
- Children present in the home
- Pregnancy
- Religious commitment
- Life satisfaction. Have the patient rate life satisfaction on a scale of 1 to 10. Life satisfaction should correspond with the patient's stated reasons for living and dying.
- Intact reality testing
- Fear of social disapproval
- Fear of suicide or death. This suggests that the patient has not yet habituated to the idea of death, a very good sign.

---

current crisis. In a very similar fashion, you can transition from the patient's symptoms to the issue of hopelessness and suicidality, normalizing the experience within the context of the psychiatric disorder. For example, when a patient is clinically depressed and anxious: *It's not unusual for someone who's been depressed and anxious to feel hopeless. Do you feel hopeless?* If hopelessness is endorsed, then you can transition to morbid ideations and eventually suicidal thinking. At each step along the way you can normalize the patient's symptoms in the context of the identified disorder. Essentially a clinical intervention, this serves to reduce anxiety and any related resistance.

What follows is an example of a hierarchical approach to this part of the interview:

Precipitant: *Can you tell me about what triggered things for you? Is there anything in particular that happened that triggered thoughts about suicide?*

Symptomatic Presentation: *Tell me about how you've been feeling lately? It sounds like you've been feeling depressed. Have you been feeling anxious, nervous, or panicky? Have you been down, low, or blue lately? Have you had trouble sleeping [additional symptoms of depression and anxiety]?*

Hopelessness: *It's not unusual for someone who's been feeling depressed to feel hopeless, like things won't change or get any better. Do you ever feel that way?*

Morbid Ruminations: *It's not unusual when you're feeling depressed and hopeless to have thoughts about death and dying. Do you ever think about death or dying?*

Suicidal Thinking: *It's not unusual when feeling depressed, hopeless, and having thoughts about death and dying to have thoughts about suicide. Have you ever thought about suicide?*

In many cases, hierarchical questioning is unnecessary, because suicidality is raised immediately by the patient or is the presenting problem. In some cases, though, a more gentle and hierarchical approach is useful. I have found this particularly true with adolescents and the elderly, populations that present unique challenges. The gradual and progressive approach to the interview reduces anxiety and associated resistance, along with facilitating the therapeutic relationship, all geared toward a more accurate risk assessment.

Much of the patient's suicidal history (predisposition to suicidal behavior) will be discussed in the context of assessing suicidal thinking. As illustrated in Table 1 (pp. 36-37), the primary areas of concern for the clinician, that is, those with empirical support, include the following:

- a previous history of psychiatric diagnoses
- previous suicide attempts, particularly multiple attempters (i.e., those at *chronic risk*)
- recent discharge from an inpatient unit
- same-sex sexual orientation
- a history of abuse (including physical, sexual, and emotional)

Those with multiple suicide attempts can be characterized as presenting chronic risk. Consistent with the construct of chronic risk, some of the latest findings indicate that those recently discharged from an inpatient unit (e.g., following suicide attempts) are at markedly greater risk in the first weeks and months following discharge, with a gradual lowering of risk over the course of the first year (Goldston et al., 1999). In short, the general idea is that a patient's acute symptoms remit during the brief inpatient stay but chronic suicide risk persists, as evidenced by subsequent attempts following discharge. This chronic risk can be exacerbated, following discharge, by a new precipitant or stressor, triggering a new suicidal crisis. Think back to the idea of lower thresholds for activation of a suicidal crisis among those with multiple attempts. It is important to monitor patients closely following discharge. Patients need more intensive follow-up and contact immediately following discharge. Recent research has also emphasized the importance of sexual orientation as a predisposing factor. Russell and Joyner (2001) have consistently found elevated suicide risk among gay, lesbian, bisexual, and transgendered individuals, with homosexual men being at highest risk.

With respect to identifiable precipitants and stressors, most can be conceptualized as losses, that is, interpersonal loss, financial loss, or identity loss. Also of importance, the clinician needs to weigh acute and chronic health problems, along with acute family disruption. Medical illnesses have been associated within increased suicide risk (American Psychiatric Association [APA], 2003). The risk is heightened when the medical illness occurs in the context of a psychiatric disorder.

In many respects, serious medical illness translates to loss: loss of autonomy and independence. All too often this loss of autonomy is both physical and financial.

Assessment and monitoring of symptomatic presentation is particularly important. The focus here is on nonpsychotic states. The decision making for suicidal patients who are acutely psychotic is straightforward: They need to be in the hospital. Naturally, the clinician needs to assess both Axis I and II diagnoses, with an eye toward comorbidity. Separate from diagnosis, it is important for the clinician to assess and monitor identifiable symptom clusters, including depression, anxiety, agitation, anger, and any associated sense of urgency. This can be done in straightforward and simple fashion by having the patient rate his or her symptoms on a 1 to 10 scale. For example, *You said you've been feeling depressed [or other symptom]. Can you rate how you're feeling now on a scale of 1 to 10, with 1 being "the best you've ever felt" and 10 being "you're so depressed you're thinking about suicide"?* The numerical ratings serve multiple purposes, including (a) improved clarity in communication between patient and clinician, (b) tracking symptom recovery over time, and (c) providing the patient with a sense of control by quantifying his or her emotional experience.

As indicated in Table 1 (pp. 36-37), the assessment of hopelessness is a separate domain. This is because of its significance in assessing suicide risk. It is not just the presence or absence of hopelessness that is important, but also its duration and severity. As evidenced in the hierarchical question sequence above, hopelessness can be assessed with a few simple questions. As with the other symptoms, I would suggest the use of a simple rating scale to track the severity of reported hopelessness over time. For example, *Can you rate your hopelessness on a scale of 1 to 10, with 1 being very hopeful and optimistic about the future and 10 being so hopeless you see suicide as the only option?* Clearly, those reporting enduring hopelessness are more likely to be multiple attempters and represent chronic risk. The previous section, "Assessing Suicidal Thinking and Behaviors," provides a detailed discussion of assessing suicidal thinking and previous suicidal behavior, integrating questions targeting reasons for living and reasons for dying. Both questions address not only intent but also the interrelated construct of hopelessness.

The assessment of impulsivity is very similar to intent in that you need to consider both subjective and objective elements. More specifically, the clinician needs to consider not just what the patient says — that is, subjective self-control — but also what the patient does, or objective self-control. Objective markers of impulsivity include substance abuse, aggression, acute interpersonal withdrawal, and sexual promiscuity. Similar to the assessment of subjective intent, you can simply ask the patient, *Do you feel in control right now?* Additional questions include:

- *Do you consider yourself an impulsive person? Why or why not?*
- *When have you felt out of control in the past?*
- *What did you do that you thought was out of control?*
- *What did you do to help yourself feel more in control?*
- *When you're feeling out of control, how long does it usually take for you to recover?*

As with intent, the clinician needs to reconcile discrepancies in self-report and what is being observed. For example: *You said you felt in control, but your behavior over the past week suggests anything but being in control: You've been intoxicated several times, drove wildly, and did other things that put you at risk. Can you explain this to me?*

The final domain to assess is protective factors. As might well be expected, social support is of central concern. Social support needs to be both available and accessible. Simple questions help assess the availability of support:

- *Do you have access to family and friends whom you can talk to and you know will be supportive?*
- *What usually happens when you ask for support [from family or friends]?*
- *Whom can you turn to in times of crisis?*
- *Are there people you need to avoid when you're feeling like this?*

The availability of support needs to be coupled with the other variables listed in Table 1 (pp. 36-37), including, in particular, a strong therapeutic relationship. As discussed previously, assessment of the patient's reasons for living is tremendously helpful in identifying not only intent, but also hopefulness. Also consider and query about close relationships such as spouse, partner, friends, and children. Similarly, expressed hopefulness about treatment, previous treatment success, religious commitment, and fear of death or dying are critical to consider. Those who express a fear of dying or self-injury have yet to habituate to the idea of suicide; this is a very good factor to emerge in the assessment process. Those at chronic risk who mention that a *fear of dying* is diminishing are at escalating risk.

POINTS TO REMEMBER FOR THE PRACTITIONER

1. Complete a comprehensive assessment for every patient where suicidality is an issue.
2. A thorough diagnostic interview and history must be completed as a part of the assessment process.
3. Always cover the targeted domains identified, including precipitants, suicidal thinking and past behavior, symptom presentation, hopelessness, impulsivity and self-control, and protective factors.
4. The use of simple 1 to 10 patient ratings are useful not only to gauge the patient's current severity across identified symptoms but also to monitor a patient's functioning and facilitate a sense of behavioral control for the patient.

PUTTING IT ALL TOGETHER: RISK FORMULATION AND RISK CATEGORIES

Rudd et al. (2004) advocated for the use of a new approach to risk categorization, identifying those at chronic high risk in addition to the more routine conceptualization of acute risk. The approach to acute risk conceptualization encouraged here represents a modification of that originally discussed by J. Somers-Flanagan and R. Somers-Flanagan (1995), integrating the terminology covered earlier. In this case, acute suicidality is believed to exist on a 5-point continuum: minimal, mild, moderate, severe, and extreme. The progression across the continuum is best indicated by escalating intent, both subjective and objective. As intent escalates, so does risk. The same can be said for symptom severity. In contrast, chronic risk is viewed as a dichotomous construct, either present or absent based on the historical information (i.e., multiple suicide attempts) available about the patient. In short, you will need to assess the acute risk for all patients, then note the presence or absence of chronic risk and the implications for immediate intervention and ongoing care.

Table 2 (p. 44) provides a summary of the various categories with indications across the assessed domains. As indicated, minimal risk communicates the absence of any active suicidal thinking. This does not mean that a patient cannot be at chronic risk. Remember, chronic risk is a historical and essentially static variable that does not change. Given the norm for day-to-day functioning for multiple attempters, those at chronic risk will most likely never be at minimal risk. It is also important to remember that patients may well be experiencing morbid ruminations that qualify them for at least mild risk if they have a previous history of suicidal ideation.

The primary reason that those with chronic suicidal problems would never be at minimal risk is that they tend to think about suicide frequently, sometimes on a predictable daily basis, and they tend to experience persistent associated symptoms. Contrary to the nonspecific thinking indicative of the mild category, those at chronic risk tend to ideate in very specific ways given the long-term nature of the problem and their previous history of suicide attempts. Similarly, their baseline symptom intensity levels are higher than the levels of those who ideate and have only made one attempt (Rudd et al., 1996).

The progression from minimal to mild risk is triggered by the emergence of suicidal thinking. The characteristic feature of mild risk is a lack of any specificity in the patient's suicidal thinking. In accordance with the mild risk label, the patient has yet to experience any specific ideations as to the how, when, and where elements of suicide. Similarly, patients in the mild category experience very limited symptoms, regardless of category (e.g., anxiety, depression, agitation) and have readily identifiable protective factors in place.

The primary difference between the mild and moderate risk categories is the emergence of specific suicidal thoughts. In other words, patients will start to think about how, when, and where they would kill themselves. Coupled with the increased specificity of the thinking, there is routinely increased frequency, duration, and subjective severity of the thoughts. To qualify as at moderate risk, the patient cannot express any intent, either subjectively or objectively. Reported symptoms continue to be mild to moderate in severity, and the patient has some noticeable protective factors.

TABLE 2: Acute Suicide Risk Continuum

Risk Level	Description
Minimal	**No identifiable suicidal ideation.** It is possible that patients with no risk will be experiencing morbid ruminations. However, if a patient is experiencing morbid ruminations, it may well be more accurate to describe him or her as at mild risk based on the severity of depressive symptoms alone.
Mild	**Suicidal ideation of limited frequency, intensity, duration, and specificity.** There are no identifiable plans, no associated intent, mild dysphoria and related symptoms, good self-control (both objective and subjective assessment), few other risk factors, and identifiable protective factors, including available and accessible social support.
Moderate	**Frequent suicidal ideation with limited intensity and duration, some specificity in terms of plans, no associated intent,** good self-control, limited dysphoria/symptomatology, some risk factors present, and identifiable protective factors, including available and accessible social support.
Severe	**Frequent, intense, and enduring suicidal ideation, specific plans, no subjective intent but some objective markers of intent (e.g., choice of lethal method(s),** the method is available/accessible, some limited preparatory behavior of some sort), evidence of impaired self-control, severe dysphoria/symptomatology, multiple risk factors present, and few if any protective factors, particularly a lack of social support.
Extreme	**Frequent, intense, and enduring suicidal ideation, specific plans, clear subjective and objective intent,** impaired self-control, severe dysphoria/symptomatology, many risk factors, and no protective factors.

As the patient moves from moderate to severe and extreme risk, several things will happen. First, there will be an emergence of intent, both subjectively and objectively. Second, symptom severity will escalate, and this will be coupled with a deterioration of protective factors. The distinction between severe and extreme risk revolves around intent. For severe risk, the patient denies subjective intent but may evidence some markers of objective intent. Once subjective intent is expressed, the patient is most accurately categorized as at extreme risk.

Let me make a quick note about the relationship between acute and chronic risk. Those with a history of multiple suicide attempts will, at best, experience acute suicidal crises that are characterized by moderate risk. The reason and rationale is really pretty straightforward. Those with a history of multiple suicide attempts tend to experience more severe and a greater breadth of symptoms and more specific suicidal thoughts in comparison to those that have made a single suicide attempt and those ideating (Rudd et al., 1996). In short, multiple attempters tend to experience more severe and enduring crises in contrast to all others. Accordingly, any time they are in acute crisis, it is most accurately described as, at a minimum, of moderate severity and risk.

Following on the heels of a thorough risk assessment interview and evaluation, the process of assigning a risk category is relatively straightforward. It is recommended that the clinician follow these steps:

1. Complete a thorough diagnostic interview, history, and suicide risk assessment (covering the risk domains identified earlier).
2. Think specifically about five critical variables: the specificity of the patient's suicidal thinking, expressed and observed intent, severity of symptoms, access to method, and available protective factors. It is important to remember that as intent and symptom severity escalate, protective factors tend to diminish.
3. Differentiate between moderate, severe, and extreme categories.
4. If subjective intent is present, the patient will be at extreme risk. If subjective intent is not present, but objective markers are present, then the patient will be at severe risk. If intent is not present, then the patient will be at moderate or lower risk. Lower risk is indicated when symptom intensity is mild and suicidal thinking is not specific.

Remember, the patient can be experiencing severe symptoms without suicidal thinking and intent and not be at severe or extreme risk. As is evident previously, the escalation of intent is critical to decision making. Keep in mind, though, that symptom severity and intent are clearly associated with one another and need to be carefully monitored in a patient with escalating symptoms.

Once risk level is assigned, it is important to share your assessment with the patient prior to discussion of your initial intervention and treatment plan. This can be accomplished in short order, for example:

> *After reviewing all the information you've provided, it looks like your risk level is best described as extreme. Let me explain why. You've reported relatively extreme and extensive symptoms of anxiety and depression, including uncontrollable panic attacks. You've also mentioned a previous history of two suicide attempts. You said that you've got a gun at home as well. What troubles me the most, though, is that not only have you been very upset, you said you have every intention of acting on the thoughts.*

A preprinted form can be found on pages 63 to 66 that can be used to organize the information from the assessment, documenting findings and risk level along with initial indications about your response. The form covers all of the relevant domains from the assessment process and also includes an area to broadly characterize the therapeutic relationship. This will help provide some context for the assessment. Given its importance in the general assessment process (and consistent with the Health Insurance Portability and Accountability Act [HIPAA]), the form also includes a mental status exam section.

The precipitants domain includes a listing of the more frequent problem areas revolving around relationships and related losses. The section on suicidal thinking prompts for several areas that are critical including preparation, rehearsal, access to means, and reasons for dying. The form also includes an area to indicate homicidal ideation. Although we have not covered homicidality as a part of our discussion, it certainly needs to be factored in as a part of the assessment and general decision-making process. The co-occurrence of suicidal and homicidal ideation is troubling, and a thorough evaluation includes questions about both (cf. Maris, Berman, & Silverman, 2004).

POINTS TO REMEMBER FOR THE PRACTITIONER

---

1. Always use a standard approach to risk assessment. This means that each and every patient will be assessed across all domains. You cannot assign risk level without a thorough assessment.
2. Be sure to cover all of the content domains summarized on pages 63 to 66.

3. Be aware of process issues in risk assessment and management. Refer back to pages 26 to 34.

4. Assign risk in accordance with escalation of intent and symptom severity.

CLINICAL DECISION MAKING AND RISK MANAGEMENT

Clinical decision making should parallel the outcome of the assessment process. Accordingly, there are measured and appropriate responses for each category of risk. As summarized in Table 3 (below), the responses are, for the most part, straightforward and relatively simple.

TABLE 3: Suicide Risk Continuum and Indicated Responses

RISK LEVEL	INDICATED RESPONSE
For All Patients	Complete a Commitment to Treatment Statement, incorporating a crisis response plan regardless of risk level. This should be a part of the informed consent process for each and every patient. Also have the patient sign the necessary release of information forms to allow for input from selected family members.
None *Mild*	No particular changes in ongoing treatment. Evaluation of any expressed suicidal ideation to monitor change in risk is needed on an ongoing basis.
Moderate	1. Recurrent evaluation of need for hospitalization 2. Increase in frequency or duration of outpatient visits 3. Active involvement of the family 4. Frequent reevaluation of treatment plan goals 5. 24-hour availability of emergency or crisis services for patient 6. Frequent reevaluation of suicide risk, noting specific changes that reduce or elevate risk 7. Consideration of medication if symptoms worsen or persist 8. Use of telephone contacts for monitoring 9. Frequent input from family members with respect to indicators 10. Professional consultation as indicated
Severe *Extreme*	Immediate evaluation for inpatient hospitalization (voluntary or involuntary, depending on situation) In cases of extreme risk, the only appropriate response is hospitalization for stabilization.

A few deserve comment and further discussion. Before discussing each category in more detail, let me first address a very important topic: the role of the no-suicide contract in managing suicidal patients. This issue is critical to management of each and every suicidal patient. Accordingly, it deserves a little more attention.

THE NO-SUICIDE CONTRACT IN CLINICAL MANAGEMENT: WHAT IS IT?

No-suicide contracts are referred to in the literature using a number of different terms, including no-harm contracts, suicide prevention contracts, no-suicide decisions, or safety agreements or contracts. Somewhat surprisingly, there does not appear to be any uniform definition of a no-suicide contract, although there clearly are common elements among most references. Nor does there appear to be any consensus as to whether such agreements must be written or verbal. More often than not, no-suicide contracts are used specifically with patients reporting suicidal thoughts or behaviors, but in some instances they have been used with all patients in the form of a broader agreement about the general nature of treatment or care, generally consistent with the notion of informed consent.

As I have stated elsewhere (Rudd, Mandrusiak, & Joiner, 2006), a no-suicide contract is an agreement between patients and clinicians in which the patients agree not to harm themselves and/or to seek help when in a suicidal state and the patient believes he or she is unable to honor the commitment. Common elements in no-suicide contracts include

- an explicit statement agreeing not to harm or kill oneself,
- specific details about the duration of the agreement,
- a contingency plan if a crisis emerges that would jeopardize the patient's ability to honor the agreement (i.e., a crisis response plan), and
- the specific responsibilities of both patient and clinician (Drew, 2001; Rudd et al., 2004).

There are a number of problems with "no-suicide contracts" that deserve more detailed discussion. Miller (1999) discussed the problem with the term "contract," identifying the hidden messages embedded in the word, noting that such language implies more concern for medicolegal aspects of practice than the clinical process. Such a contract may limit open and honest communication because patients have nothing additional to gain by signing a contract, given that such language may result in the added burden of appearing to attempt to free the clinician from blame for any bad outcome in treatment. Miller (1999) makes a compelling argument, one that indicates the term contract should be removed.

It certainly is troubling that there is no agreement about a standard definition for no-suicide contracts in the literature, but there is also a failure to provide a clear theoretical or conceptual model that articulates whether the agreement is a clinical intervention or a simple administrative procedure. A quick review of the common elements summarized earlier indicates that the agreement is a clinical intervention with several core goals that can be specifically stated and eventually empirically tested. As I have noted elsewhere (Rudd et al., 2006), these agreements hope to:

1. Facilitate honest and productive communication between the patient and therapist about suicidality by (a) making it clear what the expectations are on the part of both the clinician and patient in terms of how potentially life-threatening issues will be addressed in treatment, (b) identifying steps to follow in accessing emergency services during a crisis, (c) offering a statement of the clinical implications (e.g., more intensive care, monitoring, hospitalization) of periods during treatment characterized by heightened risk, and (d) acknowledging the control and responsibility maintained by the patient.
2. Assist in establishing and maintaining a healthy therapeutic relationship and collaborative process by articulating the need for open and honest communication and identifying the roles and responsibilities of both clinician and patient in the treatment process in general.
3. Facilitate active involvement of the patient in the treatment process, including readily accessing emergency services when and if needed.

WHAT DOES THE EMPIRICAL LITERATURE SAY ABOUT NO-SUICIDE CONTRACTS? DO THEY WORK?

Most studies targeting no-suicide contracts have simply chronicled the frequency of use, cutting across both inpatient and outpatient settings. The central finding is that the majority of inpatient facilities and outpatient practitioners working with high-risk patients use some form of no-suicide contracts (Assey, 1985; Buelow & Range, 2001; Callahan, 1996; Drew, 1999, 2000, 2001; Farrow & O'Brien, 2003; Kroll, 2000; Range et al., 2002; Simon, 1999; Weiss, 2001). It has also been noted that they are used with the greatest frequency with the highest risk patients, despite evidencing unproven efficacy.

A few studies have looked at the clinical utility of no-suicide contracts, but all face serious methodological problems. In evaluating more than 600 calls to suicide prevention centers in Canada, only 54% of verbal agreements were upheld (Mishara & Daigle, 1997). The findings have limited relevance for daily clinical practice, and adequate controls or comparisons were not in place. Drew (2001) conducted a retrospective review of medical records to assess the presence or absence of a no-suicide contract and eventual outcome. Contrary to confirming the effectiveness of the intervention, she found that patients with no-suicide contracts were more likely to engage in self-harm. Again, a central problem is the lack of adequate controls or comparison groups. Jones, O'Brien, and McMahon (1993) offered some evidence for the utility of no-suicide contracts with children, but again the study did not provide for adequate comparison groups and was not randomized. Kroll (2000) found that 41% of clinicians using no-suicide contracts had patients die by suicide or make very serious attempts while under contract. Kelly and Knudson (2000) came to a similar conclusion as that suggested here, stating that no empirical evidence supports the effectiveness of no-harm contracts in preventing suicide.

AN ALTERNATIVE FOR CLINICAL PRACTICE: THE COMMITMENT TO TREATMENT STATEMENT

I recommend the use of a commitment to treatment statement (CTS) with all suicidal patients, integrating a crisis response plan as a part of the overall agreement. The CTS is defined as an agreement between the patient and clinician in which the patient agrees to make a commitment to the treatment process and living by (a) identifying the roles, obligations, and expectations of both the clinician and patient in treatment; (b) communicating openly and honestly about all aspects of treatment including suicide; and (c) accessing identified emergency services during periods of crisis that might threaten the patient's ability to honor the agreement (Rudd et al., 2006).

The CTS does not restrict the patient's rights with respect to the option of suicide; it does not specifically mention that the patient is removing the suicide option, only that the patient is making a commitment to living by engaging in treatment and accessing emergency services if needed. I believe this is critical to the effectiveness of such agreements early in the treatment process.

It is difficult to imagine, having known the patient for only a session or two, perhaps even the first time we have met, that we would ask the patient to relinquish the right to self-determination, particularly if we have yet to actually provide anything concrete in the treatment exchange, such as symptom relief or the necessary skills for effective self-management. It is simply not realistic for a patient to make a meaningful commitment to remove suicide as an option forever during a period marked by intense psychological pain and prior to establishing a meaningful therapeutic relationship.

Without question, suicide as an option will eventually need to be addressed in treatment. This is most appropriately done after the therapeutic relationship has been firmly established, the patient has experienced some symptomatic relief, and the patient has developed adequate skills for self-management of crises (Rudd et al., 2004). We have found it useful to help the patient articulate his or her philosophy of living at the mid-point in treatment. Given the focus of this book, I will not go into any great detail about developing a philosophy of living statement; rather I refer you to previous work (Rudd et al., 2004).

CTS IN PRACTICE

It is recommended that the CTS always be handwritten and individualized by the clinician; avoid a standard preprinted form. The CTS should always include a crisis response plan, that is, the specific steps the patient should take during a crisis. Some manner of agreement should be accomplished in the first session. The implicit, and potentially problematic, messages are likely profound with use of a preprinted form.

In addition to the central elements noted above, it is also important to identify any time restrictions imposed by the patient (e.g., 1 week, 1 month, 1 year).

Here is an example of a CTS from my practice (Rudd et al., 2004; also see p. 67). It is necessarily brief and straightforward.

I, _____, agree to make a commitment to the treatment process. I understand that this means that I have agreed to be actively involved in all aspects of treatment, including

1. *attending sessions (or letting my therapist know when I can't make it),*
2. *setting goals,*
3. *voicing my opinions, thoughts, and feelings honestly and openly with my therapist (whether they are negative or positive, but most importantly my negative feelings),*
4. *being actively involved during sessions,*
5. *completing homework assignments,*
6. *taking my medications as prescribed,*
7. *experimenting with new behaviors and new ways of doings things, and*
8. *implementing my crisis response plan when needed (see the attached crisis response plan card for details).*

I also understand and acknowledge that, to a large degree, a successful treatment outcome depends on the amount of energy and effort I make. If I feel like treatment is not working, I agree to discuss it with my therapist and attempt to come to a common understanding as to what the problems are and identify potential solutions. In short, I agree to make a commitment to living. This agreement will apply for the next 3 months, at which time it will be reviewed and modified.

Signed: _____ Date: _____

Witness: _____

As should be evident, this agreement is very different from the notion of an informed consent statement. It targets the patient's motivation and commitment to the treatment process, outlining core elements and expectations. The CTS can be as brief as the one noted above or more detailed, depending on the patient and the context. In many ways, it is a living document, one that changes as the patient makes progress in treatment and the dynamics of therapy evolve.

Note that the CTS provides a signature line for a "witness." More often than not this will be a significant other or family member involved in the treatment process. It has been frequently noted that the active involvement of family is important with high-risk patients, in terms both of accomplishing accurate risk assessment and ongoing treatment and management (Rudd et al., 2004). The CTS provides a mechanism to have them understand both the significant nature of risk and the resultant management plan. I encourage clinicians to provide a copy of the CTS for the patient and encourage the patient to review and update the agreement as needed (e.g., when original time limitations are reached). A copy of the CTS should be kept in the file, as it is an integral part of the treatment record. Along these lines, I suggest it be treated as any other entry in the chart and forwarded to other providers if the clinical record is requested with a signed release. The CTS provides invaluable information on many fronts, including factors involved in the risk assessment process, risk categorization, and subsequent management decisions. Of particular importance, multiple versions of the CTS provide information as to the progression of the treatment process, crisis management strategies, the patient's compliance history, and resolution of critical issues about reasons for living and dying.

As referenced in the statement, a crisis response plan needs to be included. The crisis response plan (CRP) provides specific instructions for the patient on what to do during periods of crisis. We would suggest writing the steps down on a 3x5 card or the back of your business card (when possible). In general, the first several steps in the CRP involve self-management, in an effort to build crisis management skills. The final few steps should include external intervention, including phone contact prior to accessing the emergency room. In order for CRPs to be effective, the clinician needs to be specific about what defines a crisis, particularly for individuals who have been chronically suicidal. It is also important to practice or role-play the use of the CRP prior to implementing the agreement. The clinician may quickly discover that the plan assumes the presence of skills that are not yet adequately developed. Finally, the CRP can be modified as treatment progresses, reflecting changes in skill level and need for external intervention.

Here is an example of a CRP for someone who has been chronically suicidal, thinks about suicide daily, and can engage in self-management (see also p. 69).

Crisis Response Plan

When I'm acting on my suicidal thoughts by trying to find a gun
[or another method to kill myself], I agree to take the following steps:

Step 1: I will try to identify specifically what's upsetting me.

Step 2: Write out and review more reasonable responses to my suicidal thoughts, including thoughts about myself, others, and the future.

Step 3: Review all the conclusions I've come to about these thoughts in the past in my treatment log: For example, that the sexual abuse wasn't my fault and I don't have anything to feel ashamed of.

Step 4: Try and do the things that help me feel better for at least 30 minutes (listening to music, going to work out, calling my best friend).

Step 5: Repeat all of the above at least one more time.

Step 6: If the thoughts continue, get specific, and I find myself preparing to do something, I'll call the emergency call person at (phone number: _____).

Step 7: If I still feel suicidal and don't feel like I can control my behavior, I'll go to the emergency room located at: _____ _____ (phone number: _____).

It might be helpful to provide a brief example of how the CTS (and CRP) are introduced in the clinical exchange. What follows is a brief transcript about how to introduce the CTS (Rudd et al., 2006).

Therapist: Since we've now discussed many of the problems that brought you here, including your thoughts about suicide, I'd like for us to come to some agreement about how treatment will work and what steps you'll take if another crisis emerges. How does that sound?

Patient: I'm not really sure what you mean.

Therapist: Well, I'd like to put down on paper what I like to call a Commitment to Treatment Statement outlining what is expected of both you and I in treatment. For example, how often you'll be coming to treatment, how long the sessions will last, what we will actually be doing when you're here, and what you'll do if you experience a crisis. The last item

I call a crisis response plan. If okay, I'd like to write out the Commitment to Treatment Statement on a sheet of paper and have both you and I sign it. I'll put the crisis response plan on the back of my business card (when possible) so you can just put it in your wallet when you need it. I'd also like to have your wife sign the agreement since we'll be enlisting her help during treatment.

Patient: Actually I like the idea. I'd feel much better if I knew how things were going to work and what exactly I was supposed to do if I get in trouble and start thinking about killing myself again.

Therapist: As a part of this agreement, I'll be asking you to make a commitment to living; by that I mean that you're agreeing to being involved in treatment and accessing emergency services when needed. How long do you think you could make such a commitment right now? Could you agree to 6 months or longer?

Patient: I'd feel comfortable with 3 months right now.

Therapist: Then after 3 months we'll sit down and evaluate how things have gone and draft a new agreement at that time. I'm going to go ahead and start writing while we talk. One thing to remember is that this agreement can change if needed. All you need to do is let me know what things need to be modified. After we finish, I'll keep a copy and give one to you as well. Okay, I'm making a note that this will last for 3 months and that we'll review at that time. Let's go through the things that will be involved in treatment.

ENLISTING THE HELP OF FAMILY MEMBERS

It is important to enlist the help of family members in crisis management and ongoing care. This can be accomplished by incorporating this expectation into the CTS, as well as the crisis response plan. When doing so, it is always of critical importance to make certain that the family member (spouse, parent, sibling, etc.) has a healthy relationship with the patient. The family member serves as a contact point during periods of crisis and related home monitoring, as well as an additional resource for information about how the patient is functioning on a day-to-day basis. Early in the assessment and treatment process, integration of a family member requires the patient to sign the appropriate release of information forms. I have the patient do this well in advance of a crisis, clarifying in detail that I will contact the family member for assistance in home monitoring during periods of crisis and that we may also have the family member come in for joint sessions during the assessment process.

As mentioned at the beginning of this section, crisis management is straightforward and simply follows the risk assessment. When severe or extreme risk levels are present, the only alternative is to evaluate the patient for hospitalization. In cases where the patient is evaluated and referred, but not hospitalized, it is incumbent on the clinician to reevaluate the patient, clarify if the risk level has dropped, and, if not, refer the patient again for hospitalization. As indicated in Table 3 (p. 47), the "moderate" category offers the most flexibility. One intervention that I have found particularly useful is telephone monitoring. This involves setting aside a standard time each day for the patient to call and "check in," allowing you to monitor any fluctuations in risk level (particularly elevations that would require hospitalization). It is important to note that I use this only with patients I know well. Also, it needs to be made clear to patients that if they do not call in at the designated time, you will attempt to reach them, but if unsuccessful you will call the police, assuming that it is an emergency situation. Telephone monitoring allows the patient to have brief daily contact with the clinician, avoid unnecessary hospitalization, and retain independence in an effort to reduce acute symptoms.

POINTS TO REMEMBER FOR THE PRACTITIONER

1. Use a Commitment to Treatment Statement with all suicidal patients. Actually, I would suggest using the CTS with all patients, regardless of whether or not they are suicidal. Be concrete. Identify the patient's responsibilities in specific detail, along with your own.
2. Always include a crisis response plan with the CTS.
3. Be sure to make the crisis response plan concrete, with a clear definition of what is considered a crisis. Always

rehearse or practice the crisis response plan to make sure that it is something the patient can implement and the skill level is not too advanced.

4. When possible, include family members in the assessment and management process. Be sure to have them sign the appropriate release of information forms at the very beginning; do not wait until a crisis.

THE IMPORTANCE OF DOCUMENTATION: OPEN AND CLOSED RISK MARKERS

As evidenced in the last section, suicide risk assessment is about recognizing and responding to markers of risk. The framework provided here discusses the need to address both acute and chronic variables. Perhaps the easiest and most effective way to think about suicide risk is to understand that each and every time you identify a marker of risk in the chart (i.e., you have documented it in writing), you have opened a marker of risk. That open marker will need to be addressed in subsequent entries until it is either effectively resolved or of minimal consequence in the clinical scenario. This is essentially what expert forensic reviewers do when reviewing a chart in which there has been a negative outcome, that is, a suicide or suicide attempt.

Perhaps the easiest way to apply this approach is to take a chart of a previous suicidal patient. You can take out a sheet of paper and draw a line down the middle, giving yourself two columns. Label one "open markers" and the other "date closed." Then you can go through your chart indicating those variables you identified as important in elevating the patient's suicide risk. Once you have an exhaustive list of all variables you linked to suicide risk, you can then go back through the chart and identify the dates of entries indicating when the problem was effectively addressed and resolved. Failure to address identified risk variables is the foundation of negligence and malpractice claims. This simple exercise will help you understand why clinicians can increase their liability purely as a function of documentation rather than the nature and quality of clinical care provided.

I provided a standard preprinted form on pages 63 to 66. Regardless of whether you choose to use this form or create your own (which is entirely appropriate), I would encourage you to consider the importance of two issues. First is the importance of differentiating acute and chronic risk for suicide. I believe the argument for doing this is compelling given the emerging empirical foundation. Second is the need to close all open markers of risk. Although it may sound a little defensive in nature, the open-closed marker approach to risk assessment and management leads to not only greater clarity in the risk assessment process, but also better clinical care. It will force you to monitor more closely those variables you previously identified as most important and respond to them in timely fashion in the clinical environment.

> ## POINTS TO REMEMBER FOR THE PRACTITIONER

1. Always "close" open markers of risk.
2. Review your charts for open and closed markers of risk.

CONSULTATION: KNOWING WHEN TO ASK FOR HELP

The importance of ready and knowledgeable consultation cannot be overstated. Each and every practicing clinician needs to identify and have at the ready a list of colleagues who can provide short-notice consultation for cases of suicidality. There are several things to remember about clinical consultation in this area and they are listed below.

> ## POINTS TO REMEMBER FOR THE PRACTITIONER

1. First is that it is essential. Consultation serves many purposes, just one of which is to review the clinical indicators of risk and related management decisions. In addition, appropriate clinical consultation allows the clinician to identify and respond to any troublesome countertransference issues.
2. Always document the consultation. Be sure to document the issues addressed and any related confirmation or questions raised by the consultant.

3. Inform your consultant that you are requesting "formal" consultation that will be documented. Some have raised concerns about shared liability in these cases, but there is yet to be a clearly articulated standard here.

4. Have a standard approach to the requested consultation, presenting and reviewing the case in a set fashion, incorporating the risk assessment framework provided. Remember, good consultation is only possible if clear and accurate information is presented.

CLOSING COMMENTS: CLINICAL PRACTICE AND THE REALITY OF SUICIDE

Although the possibility of suicide is undoubtedly one of the more anxiety-provoking scenarios in clinical practice, the reality is that it is a relatively infrequent event. Over the course of a career, it is estimated that a fourth to a third of clinicians will experience the suicide of a patient. Coupled with this fear is that of being sued or facing professional complaints of negligence or incompetence. In recognition of these worries, many organizations have recently offered specific guidance to the practicing clinician. The American Psychiatric Association (APA, 2003) recently published practice guidelines for suicide risk assessment. Similarly, the American Association of Suicidology (2005) recently formed a multidisciplinary working group to address the issue of "core competencies" in the assessment and management of suicidality.

The utilization of a common assessment framework by no means guarantees that one of our patients will not die by suicide. Rather, it guarantees that we will do our assessments in accordance with the best available practice standards and empirical evidence. A standard framework helps ensure that each and every patient will undergo a thorough and detailed assessment, rendering accurate information to guide clinical decisions. This is the simple reality of clinical practice. There are recognizable and significant limitations to what we control in the clinical environment.

It is important for clinicians to acknowledge this limitation of control from the outset and focus accordingly on what we do control.

We control the thoroughness of the risk assessment framework employed. We control the process variables involved in the risk assessment process, at least from our end. We control the subsequent risk formulation and recommended clinical response. We control whether we attempt to implement our recommendations and whether we follow up with the patient. We control how well we document all of the above. Let us focus on what we know and what we can influence in the clinical context. In doing so, we will undoubtedly save lives!

<u>APPENDICES</u>

Appendix A

Standard Suicide Risk Assessment Form

A comprehensive suicidality assessment was conducted due to (check one about the nature of the referral):

___ Referral source identified suicidal symptoms or risk factors
___ Patient reported suicidal thoughts/feelings on intake paperwork/ assessment tools *(please attach a copy of the assessment instrument with applicable items circled)*
___ Patient reported suicidal thoughts/feelings during the intake interview
___ Recent event already occurred (circle appropriate: suicide attempt / suicide threat)
___ Other: _____
_____

Describe the therapeutic alliance/relationship at the end of the initial session (circle appropriate answer)**:**

Poor---------------------Routine---------------------Good

If Poor, please indicate problems observed and response by therapist:
_____
_____

In the following sections, circle Y for "yes" and N for "no" and provide accompanying details.

Precipitants to Consider:

Y N Significant Loss
Describe: _____

Y N Interpersonal Isolation
Describe: _____

Y N Relationship Problems
Describe: _____

Y N Health Problems
Describe: _____

Y N Legal Problems
Describe: _____

Y N Other Problems
Describe: _____

Nature of Suicidal Thinking:

Y   N   Suicide Ideation

- Frequency: Never   Rarely   Sometimes   Frequently   Daily
- Intensity: (Mild) 1   2   3   4   5   6   7   8   9   10   (Severe)
  Other: _____
- Duration: _____ Seconds   _____ Minutes   _____Hours

Y   N   Current Intent

- Subjective reports (provide quote): _____
  _____
- Objective signs (behaviors): _____
  _____

Y   N   Suicide Plan

- When: _____
- Where: _____
- How: _____
          Y   N   Access to means

Y   N   Suicide Preparation: _____
Y   N   Suicide Rehearsal: _____
          Reasons for Dying: _____
          _____

History of Suicidal Behavior:

Y   N   History of Suicidality

- Ideation: _____
- Single Attempt: _____
- Multiple Attempts: _____

Symptom Severity (fill in appropriate rating):

Depression: Rating (1-10) _____
Anxiety: Rating (1-10) _____
Anger: Rating (1-10) _____
Agitation: Rating (1-10) _____

Onset of symptom clusters: _____
Duration of symptom clusters: _____

Hopelessness (fill in appropriate rating):

Rating (1-10): _____
Onset: _____
Duration: _____

Impulsivity/Self-Control:

Y   N   Impulsivity
- Subjective reports: _____
- Objective signs: _____

_____

Y   N   Substance abuse – Describe: _____

_____

Additional Factors to Consider:

Y   N   Homicidal ideation – Describe: _____

_____

Additional risk factors (check all that apply):

☐ Age over 60 ☐ Male ☐ Previous Axis I or II psychiatric diagnosis
☐ Previous history of suicidal behavior   ☐ Family history of suicide
☐ Homosexual orientation   ☐ Access to firearms
☐ History of physical, emotional, or sexual abuse

Mental Status (circle all that apply):

Alertness: alert / drowsy / lethargic / stuporous
                Other: _____

Oriented to: person / place / time / reason for evaluation

Mood: euthymic / elevated / dysphoric / agitated / angry

Affect: flat / blunted / constricted / appropriate / labile

Thought   clear and coherent / goal-directed / tangential / circumstantial
Continuity: Other: _____

Thought   Within normal limits (WNL) / obsessions / delusions /
Content: ideas of reference / bizarreness / morbidity
                Other: _____

Abstraction: WNL / notably concrete
                Other: _____

Speech: WNL / rapid / slow / slurred / impoverished / incoherent
                Other: _____

Memory: grossly intact
                Other: _____

Reality   WNL
Testing: Other: _____

Notable Behavioral Observations:_____

_____

Rating of Acute Risk (circle appropriate category):

 None-----Mild-----Moderate-----Severe-----Extreme

Presence/Absence of Chronic Risk (circle appropriate category):

Absent-----Present

If present, summarize markers of chronic risk: _____

_____

_____

_____

DSM-IV-TR Diagnosis:

 Axis I:

 Axis II:

 Axis III:

 Axis IV:

 Axis V:

Plan: At the current time, outpatient care **can / cannot** (circle one) provide sufficient safety and stability. Safety plan includes the following:

 1. _____

 2. _____

 3. _____

 4. _____

Patient agrees to this plan: Y / N

Patient was provided a written **crisis response plan**: Y / N

Patient was provided a commitment to treatment statement: Y / N

Appendix B

Sample Commitment to
<u>Treatment Statement (CTS)</u>

I, _____, *agree to make a commitment to
the treatment process. I understand that this means that I have agreed to
be actively involved in all aspects of treatment, including*

1. *attending sessions (or letting my therapist know when I can't make it),*
2. *setting goals,*
3. *voicing my opinions, thoughts, and feelings honestly and openly with my therapist (whether they are negative or positive, but most importantly my negative feelings),*
4. *being actively involved during sessions,*
5. *completing homework assignments,*
6. *taking my medications as prescribed,*
7. *experimenting with new behaviors and new ways of doings things, and*
8. *implementing my crisis response plan when needed (see the attached crisis response plan card for details).*

*I also understand and acknowledge that, to a large degree, a successful
treatment outcome depends on the amount of energy and effort I make. If
I feel like treatment is not working, I agree to discuss it with my therapist
and attempt to come to a common understanding as to what the problems
are and identify potential solutions. In short, I agree to make a commitment
to living. This agreement will apply for the next 3 months, at which time it
will be reviewed and modified.*

Signed: _____ *Date:* _____

Witness: _____

Appendix C

Sample Crisis Response Plan (CRP)

When I'm acting on my suicidal thoughts by trying to find a gun [or another method to kill myself], I agree to take the following steps:

Step 1: I will try to identify specifically what's upsetting me.

Step 2: Write out and review more reasonable responses to my suicidal thoughts, including thoughts about myself, others, and the future.

Step 3: Review all the conclusions I've come to about these thoughts in the past in my treatment log: For example, that the sexual abuse wasn't my fault and I don't have anything to feel ashamed of.

Step 4: Try and do the things that help me feel better for at least 30 minutes (listening to music, going to work out, calling my best friend).

Step 5: Repeat all of the above at least one more time.

Step 6: If the thoughts continue, get specific, and I find myself preparing to do something, I'll call the emergency call person at (phone number: _____).

Step 7: If I still feel suicidal and don't feel like I can control my behavior, I'll go to the emergency room located at:

_____

(phone number: _____).

REFERENCES

American Association of Suicidology. (2005). *Clinical Skills Core Competencies Curriculum (for Mental Health Professionals Working With Individuals at Risk for Suicide)*. Washington, DC: Author.

American Psychiatric Association. (2003). Practice guideline for the assessment and treatment of patients with suicidal behaviors. *Official Journal of the American Psychiatric Association, 160*(11 Suppl.), 1-60.

Assey, J. L. (1985). The suicide prevention contract. *Perspectives in Psychiatric Care, 23*, 99-103.

Bender, D. S. (2005). The therapeutic alliance in the treatment of personality disorders. *Journal of Psychiatric Practice, 11*(2), 73-87.

Bongar, B. (Ed.). (1991). *The Suicidal Patient: Clinical and Legal Standards of Care*. Washington, DC: American Psychological Association.

Bongar, B. (Ed.). (1992). *Suicide: Guidelines for Assessment, Management, and Treatment*. New York: Oxford University Press.

Bongar, B., Peterson, L. G., Harris, E. A., & Aissis, J. (1989). Clinical and legal considerations in the management of suicidal patients: An integrative overview. *Journal of Integrative and Eclectic Psychotherapy, 8*(1), 53-67.

Brown, G. K. (2001). *A Review of Suicide Assessment Measures for Intervention Research With Adults and Older Adults*. Unpublished manuscript.

Buelow, G., & Range, L. M. (2001). The suicide prevention contract. *Perspectives in Psychiatric Care, 23*, 99-103.

Callahan, J. (1996). Documentation of client dangerousness in a managed care environment. *Health and Social Work, 21*, 202-207.

Clark, D., & Fawcett, J. (1992). Review of empirical risk factors for evaluation of the suicidal patient. In B. Bongar (Ed.), *Suicide: Guidelines for Assessment, Management, and Treatment* (pp. 16-48). New York: Oxford University Press.

Drew, B. L. (1999). No-suicide contracts to prevent suicidal behavior in inpatient psychiatric settings. *Journal of the American Psychiatric Nurses Association, 5*, 23-28.

Drew, B. L. (2000). Suicidal behavior and no-suicide contracts in inpatient psychiatric settings. *Dissertation Abstracts International: Section B: The Sciences and Engineering, 60*(11-B), 5428.

Drew, B. L. (2001). Self-harm behavior and no-suicide contracting in psychiatric inpatient settings. *Archives of Psychiatric Nursing, 15*(3), 99-106.

Farrow, T. L., & O'Brien, A. J. (2003). No-suicide contracts and informed consent: An analysis of ethical issues. *Nursing Ethics, 10*, 199-207.

Forman, E. M., Berk, M. S., Henriques, G. R., Brown, G. K., & Beck, A. T. (2004). History of multiple suicide attempts as a behavioral marker of severe psychopathology. *American Journal of Psychiatry, 161*(3), 437-443.

Gaston, L., Thompson, L., Gallagher, D., Cournoyer, L-G, & Gagnon, R. (1998). Alliance, technique, and their interactions in predicting outcome of behavioral, cognitive, and brief dynamic therapy. *Psychotherapy Research, 8*(2), 190-209.

Goldston, D. B. (2003). *Measuring Suicidal Behavior and Risk in Children and Adolescents*. Washington, DC: American Psychological Association.

Goldston, D. B., Daniel, S. S., Reboussin, D. M., Reboussin, B. A., Frazier, P. H., & Kelley, A. E. (1999). Suicide attempts among formerly hospitalized adolescents: A prospective naturalistic study of risk during the first 5 years after discharge. *Journal of the American Academy of Child and Adolescent Psychiatry, 38*, 660-671.

Gould, M. S., Marrocco, F. A., Kleinman, M., Thomas, J. G., Mostkoff, K., Cote, J., & Davies, M. (2005). Evaluating iatrogenic risk of youth suicide screening programs. *Journal of the American Medical Association, 293*(13), 1635-1643.

Jobes, D. A. (2000). Collaborating to prevent suicide: A clinical-research perspective. *Suicide and Life-Threatening Behavior, 30*(1), 8-17.

Jobes, D. A., & Berman, A. L. (1993). Suicide and malpractice liability: Assessing and revising policies, procedures, and practice in outpatient settings. *Professional Psychology: Research and Practice, 24*, 91-99.

Jobes, D. A., & Maltsberger, J. T. (1995). The hazards of treating suicidal patients. In M. Sussman (Ed.), *A Perilous Calling: The Hazards of Psychotherapy Practice* (pp. 200-214). New York: John Wiley.

Joiner, T. E., Jr., Conwell, Y., Fitzpatrick, K., Witte, T., Schmidt, B., Berlin, M., Fleck, P., & Rudd, M. D. (2005). Four studies on the immutability of the association between past and subsequent suicidality: Covary "everything but the kitchen sink." *Journal of Abnormal Psychology, 114*(2), 291-303.

Jones, R. N., O'Brien, P., & McMahon, W. M. (1993). Contracting to lower precaution status for child psychiatric patients. *Journal of Psychosocial Nursing, 31*, 6-10.

Kelly, K .T., & Knudson, M. P. (2000). Are no-suicide contracts effective in preventing suicide in suicidal patients seen by primary care physicians? *Archives of Family Medicine, 9*, 1119-1121.

Kroll, J. (2000). Use of no-suicide contracts by psychiatrists in Minnesota. *American Journal of Psychiatry, 157*, 1684-1686.

Linehan, M. M. (1993). *Cognitive-Behavioral Treatment of Borderline Personality Disorder*. New York: Guilford.

Litman, R. (1989). Suicides: What do they have in mind? In D. Jacobs & H. N. Brown (Eds.), *Suicide: Understanding and Responding* (pp. 143-156). Madison, CT: International Universities Press.

Maltsberger, J. T. (1986). *Suicide Risk: The Formulation of Clinical Judgment*. New York: University Press.

Maltsberger, J. T., & Buie, D. H. (1974). Countertransference hate in the treatment of suicidal patients. *Archives of General Psychiatry, 30*(5), 625-633.

Maltsberger, J. T., & Buie, D. H. (1989). Common errors in the management of suicidal patients. In D. Jacobs & H. N. Brown (Eds.), *Suicide: Understanding and Responding* (pp. 285-294). Madison, CT: International Universities Press.

Maris, R. W. (1992). The relationship of nonfatal suicide attempts to completed suicide. In R. Maris, A. Berman, J. Maltsberger, & R. Yufit (Eds.), *Assessment and Prediction of Suicide* (pp. 362-380). New York: Guilford.

Maris, R. W., Berman, A. L., Maltsberger, J. T., & Yufit, R. I. (Eds.). (1992). *Assessment and Prediction of Suicide*. New York: Guilford.

Maris, R. W., Berman, A. L., & Silverman, M. M. (2004). *Comprehensive Textbook of Suicidology*. New York: Guilford.

Miller, M. C. (1999). Suicide-prevention contracts. In D. G. Jacobs (Ed.), *The Harvard Medical School Guide to Suicide Assessment and Intervention*. San Francisco: Jossey-Bass.

Mishara, B. L., & Daigle, M. (1997). Effects of different telephone intervention styles with suicidal callers at two suicide prevention centers: An empirical investigation. *American Journal of Community Psychology, 25*, 861-885.

Motto, J. (1979). The psychopathology of suicide: A clinical approach. *American Journal of Psychiatry, 136*(4-B), 516-520.

O'Carroll, P., Berman, A., Maris, R., Moscicki, E., Tanney, B., & Silverman, M. (1996). Beyond the Tower of Babel: A nomenclature for suicidology. *Suicide and Life-Threatening Behavior, 26*, 237-252.

Pokorny, A. (1992). Prediction of suicide in psychiatric patients: Report of a prospective study. In R. Maris, A. Berman, J. Maltsberger, & R. Yufit (Eds.), *Assessment and Prediction of Suicide* (pp. 105-129). New York: Guilford.

Pope, K. S., & Tabachnick, B. G. (1993). Therapists' anger, hate, fear, and sexual feelings: National survey of therapist responses, client characteristics, critical events, formal complaints, and training. *Professional Psychology: Research and Practice, 24*(2), 142-152.

Range, L. J., Campbell, C., Kovac, S. H., Marion-Jones, M., Aldridge, H., Kogos, S., & Crump, Y. (2002). No-suicide contracts: An overview and recommendations. *Death Studies, 26*, 51-74.

Rudd, M. D. (2006). Fluid vulnerability theory: A cognitive approach to understanding the process of acute and chronic suicide risk (pp. 355-368). In T. Ellis (Ed.), *Cognition and Suicide: Theory, Research, and Therapy*. Washington, DC: American Psychological Association.

Rudd, M. D., Joiner, T. E., Jr., Jobes, D. A., & King, C. A. (1999). The outpatient treatment of suicidality: An integration of science and recognition of its limitations. *Professional Psychology: Research and Practice 30*(5), 437-446.

Rudd, M. D., Joiner, T. E., Jr., & Rajab, H. (1995). Help negation after acute suicidal crisis. *Journal of Consulting and Clinical Psychology, 63*(3), 499-503.

Rudd, M. D., Joiner, T. E., Jr., & Rajab, H. (1996). Relationships among suicide ideators, attempters, and multiple attempters in a young adult sample. *Journal of Abnormal Psychology, 105*, 541-550.

Rudd, M. D., Joiner, T. E., Jr., & Rajab, H. (2004). *Treating Suicidal Behavior.* New York: Guilford.

Rudd, M. D., Mandrusiak, M., & Joiner, T. E., Jr. (2006). The case against no-suicide contracts: The commitment to treatment statement as a practice alternative. *Journal of Clinical Psychology, 62*(2), 243-251.

Russell, S. T., & Joyner, K. (2001). Adolescent sexual orientation and suicide risk: Evidence from a national study. *American Journal of Public Health, 91*, 1276-1281.

Shneidman, E. (1981). Psychotherapy with suicidal patients. *Suicide and Life-Threatening Behavior, 11*(4), 341-348.

Shneidman, E. (1984). Aphorisms of suicide and some implications for psychotherapy. *American Journal of Psychotherapy, 38*(3), 319-328.

Simon, R. I. (1999). The suicide prevention contract: Clinical, legal, and risk management issues. *Journal of the American Academy of Psychiatry and the Law, 27*, 445-450.

Somers-Flanagan, J., & Somers-Flanagan, R. (1995). Intake interviewing with suicidal patients: A systematic approach. *Professional Psychology: Research and Practice, 26*, 41-47.

Weiss, A. (2001). The no-suicide contract: Possibilities and pitfalls. *American Journal of Psychotherapy, 55*, 414-419.

If You Found This Book Useful . . .

You might want to know about our other titles.

If you would like to receive our latest catalog, please return this form:

Name: _____
(Please Print)

Address: _____

Address: _____

City/State/Zip: _____
This is ❑ home ❑ office

Telephone: (_____) _____

E-mail: _____

Fax: (_____) _____

I am a:

❑ Psychologist   ❑ Mental Health Counselor
❑ Psychiatrist   ❑ Marriage and Family Therapist
❑ School Psychologist   ❑ Not in Mental Health Field
❑ Clinical Social Worker   ❑ Other: _____

◆   ◆   ◆

Professional Resource Press
P.O. Box 3197
Sarasota, FL 34230-3197

Telephone: 800-443-3364
FAX: 941-343-9201
E-Mail: cs.prpress@gmail.com
website: www.prpress.com

AMS/5/13

Add A Colleague To Our Mailing List . . .

If you would like us to send our latest catalog to one of your colleagues, please return this form:

Name: _____
(Please Print)

Address: _____

Address: _____

City/State/Zip: _____
This is ☐ home ☐ office

Telephone: (_____) _____

E-mail: _____

Fax: (_____) _____

This person is a:

☐ Psychologist   ☐ Mental Health Counselor
☐ Psychiatrist   ☐ Marriage and Family Therapist
☐ School Psychologist   ☐ Not in Mental Health Field
☐ Clinical Social Worker   ☐ Other: _____

Name of person completing this form: _____

◆   ◆   ◆

Professional Resource Press
P.O. Box 3197
Sarasota, FL 34230-3197

Telephone: 800-443-3364
FAX: 941-343-9201
E-Mail: cs.prpress@gmail.com
website: www.prpress.com

AMS/5/13